Renaissance of Butterflies

Angel Ramos

Copyright © 2019 Angel Ramos

All rights reserved. No part(s) of this book may be reproduced, distributed or transmitted in any form, or by any means, or stored in a database or retrieval systems without prior expressed written permission of the author of this book.

ISBN: 978-1-5356-1692-8

This book is dedicated to

FCSA

Fibromyalgia Care Society of America

2 really define the true meaning
of reality of n understanding
that being in the PERSENT!

+ + +

love my self,respect
my self,value my self ,
with the understanding
of having self per..second!

+ + +

Self say,
self who walk with me
shall not feel the darkness.
 self shall feel the light,
Self who feel the light
hear the MUSIC!!!!................. born 2 b

+ + +

love myself , respect my self,
and value my self
that what is always on thy mind .
apply what called understanding...
 blessin 2 thy n those

+ + +

Angel Ramos

ESSENCE OF TIME IS UNDERSTANDING.
THE PRESENT 2 DEFINE
WHAT IT TRUELYTHE BEING WITH SELF ,
AT THE MONENT OF NOW

✦ ✦ ✦

Observation is what u see,
learn 2 look at self ,
NOW can u see
that without the mirror!!

✦ ✦ ✦

life is like a rose ,
watch out 4 the thorn ,
which r call emotion

✦ ✦ ✦

word start with letter,
emotion start with words
b-careful of one second

✦ ✦ ✦

JOURNEY CAN B MADE,
JUS FOLLOW YR HEART!!!!!!

✦ ✦ ✦

THE KEYS 2 REALITY
IS UNDERSTANDING
THY EMOTIONS!!!!!
THE POWER IS IN YOU ,
CALLED SIMPLE

❖ ❖ ❖

DURING A LIFE TIME,
WE TURN OVER ALOTS OF STONE.
THAT BECAME PROBLEM 4 OURSELF,
THERE WAS A STONE WE SEEN.
BUT NEVER TURN THAT SPECAIL STONE.
LADY N GENTLEMENT THAT STONE
WAS ALWAYS THERE STONE
IT CALLED SELF!!!
HOLD THAT STONE IN YR HEART..

❖ ❖ ❖

there r oceans
n there r emotions.
which one of these 2
can b a danger 2 1self!!!!!

❖ ❖ ❖

DONT LET YR PAST
B YR FUTURE,
CAUSE U MISS
THE PRESENT BLESSIN

Angel Ramos

✦ ✦ ✦

being is simple
jus smile……..

✦ ✦ ✦

REALIATY IS LIKE AN ADVENTURE ,
ONCE U EXPERIENCE
U WOULD LOVE BEING IT

✦ ✦ ✦

WORK is a place that
we have 2 adopt 2 n that's self.
That where the real work
come in define
 that's in I

✦ ✦ ✦

like i said i guarantee……..
 awesome with yr surrounding
with yr SELF

✦ ✦ ✦

emotions create dark,
understanding create the light

that's the path 2 see
our inner being of experience

✦ ✦ ✦

the birth of 1 self ,
no matter wat age
is the path 2 enlightenment
of understanding of 1 self.

✦ ✦ ✦

IF can see nothing,
welcome aboard you
are in the right path
to understanding thy self..

✦ ✦ ✦

LOVE ALWAYS OUTWEIGH PAIN ,
UNTIL EMOTIONS R CREATED
BY SELF N FED BY THE MIND................
B-CAREFUL!

✦ ✦ ✦

NOTHING IS THE ROAD TO EVERYTHING

TEARS R LIKE LIFE,
WE HAVE PAIN,
DARKNESS, EMPTYNESS VIODS.
BUT IF WE LOOK AT IT,
THERE ARE JOY,4FILMENT,
LOVE, RESPECT, VALUE, N UNDERSTANDING.
LEARN 2 READ YR TEAR
DONT LET YR TEAR READ U,,,,,,,,,,
UNDERSTANDING THY SELF!!

♦ ♦ ♦

MAY THE CHAMBERS OF MADNESS B TAME,
BY THE PLEASURE OF LAUGHTER!!!!!!!!!......................SMILE...

♦ ♦ ♦

DARKNESS CAN SEE
THE LIGHT
IF WE INVERT IT.....
UNDERSTANDING.

♦ ♦ ♦

MAY THE LOVE OF THE MYTH,
DEFINE THE UNDERSTANDING

THE PURE ESSENCE,,,,,,,,,,,,,,,,,,,,,,,,SELF!!!!!!!!!!

✦ ✦ ✦

WHATS A GIFT ,
A GIFT IS SOMETHING
THAT ALWAYS WAS THERE.
BUT WE NEVER LOOK AT IT,
WE LOOK AT EVERYTHING
THATS INFRONT OF US
BUT WE NEVER SEEN THAT GIFT.
UNDERSTANDING THAT
THAT GIFT ALWAYS MENT SELF.
SELF GIFT U EVERTHING
 U NEEED IN LIFE ,
LIKE LOVE RESPECT, VALUE

✦ ✦ ✦

WE CREATE POSITIVE
BY FOCUSING ON SELF!
 IT CALL BEING AWARE OF 1SELF
AT THE MOMENTS
AS NOW,NOW,NOW,NOW

✦ ✦ ✦

MAY OUR BLESSIN
KEEP PRESENTING IT SELF ALWAYS!!!
PEACE IS ALWAYS THE GUIDE
BEING IS JUS BEING,SIMPLE

JUS B WITH LOVE.
HARD BUT UNDERSTANDING,,,,,
BLESS THY SELF

✦ ✦ ✦

THE VOICE OF THE ANSWER,
IS THE QUESTION OF THE HEART

✦ ✦ ✦

A BLESSIN IS EVERYTHING
THAT WE BECOME EVERY SECOND.
SOOOO BECOME THAT SECOND,
NOW, NOW, NOW

✦ ✦ ✦

MAY BLESSIN ALWAYS B THE PATH,
IN THE POWER 2 B
CREATE WHAT IS PRESENT IN WORDS

✦ ✦ ✦

MAY BLESSIN ALWAYS B THE PATH,
IN THE POWER 2 B

THERE IS ALWAYS A NEW HERIZON
B4 OUR DECISION IS MADE.
THAT HERIZON IT WITH LOVE,
RESPECT, VALUE,,HAPPINESS,
4FULLMMENT, JOY, SECURE, AWARENESS.
BEING AWARE OF THE HERIZON
OUR PATH 2 OUR DECISION WILL B BLESS!!!!

✦ ✦ ✦

PEOPLE LOOK 4 RICHNESS IN   EVERYTHING,
BUT WE 4GET THAT THE TRUE
RICHNESS IS WITH IN OUR WORDS
THAT DEFINE OUR UNDERSTANDING SELF

✦ ✦ ✦

TEAR CRY AMONG THEMSELF,
WHEN THEY SEE THE PAIN IN OTHERS
,,,,,,,,,,,,,,,,,,,,,,,,,,,MIRROR, MIRROR,

✦ ✦ ✦

THE ESSENCE IS THE LIGHT IN YR PATH, THAT (U) R

IF WE CAN 4FILL
LIGHTNESS WITH PAIN.
WHY WE CAN'T 4FILL
DARKNESS WITH JOY!!!!!
WHY, WHY, WHY

Angel Ramos

✦ ✦ ✦

YEARS, MONTHS, DAYS,
SUMMERS, WINTERS, SPRINGS, FALLS,
DAYS AND NIGHTS,
HOT AND COLD,
HOURS, MINUTES, AND SECONDS.
WHEN U LOOK AT THIS,
 U MAY THINK ITS ALL DIFFERENT.
NOPE!! IT JUST A SIMPLE WORD
CALL TIME.
BUT WE MAKE IT 2 COMPLEX.
SIMPLE DEFINE SELF,
 AND U DEFINE TIME
IN THE PRESENT OF WORDS

✦ ✦ ✦

 BY UNDERSTANDING WE CAN CHOOSE
THE RIGHT WORDS 2 DEFINE
 OUR INNER BEING OF TRUTH
IF WORDS CAN CREATE UNDERSTANDING,
WHY CAN UNDERSTANDING CREATE UNDERSTANDING
,,,,,,,,,,,THINK

✦ ✦ ✦

MAY THE BLESSIN
 WALK THERE PATH,
AS THEIR SECONDS,

ENJOY THEIR DAY
YES 2-DAY !!!!!! HUMBLE

❖ ❖ ❖

NO MATTER IF THE ANSWER
2 THE QUESTION IS WRONG,
WE DONT HAVE THE RITE,
2 LET THE EMOTIONAL
AFFECT OF THE ANSWER
GET THE BEST OF YR SELF!!

❖ ❖ ❖

EMOTIONS SAY SHOW ME THE PAIN
N I WILL SHOW U THE DARKNESS,
UNDERSTANDING SAY
SHOW ME THE JOY OF SELF
N I WILL GIVE U
THE PATH 2 THE LIGHT
.............A GUIDE 2 U.

THE FORCES OF NATURE:
PAIN, ANGER, VIOD, EMPTYNESS,
DARKNESS, LONLINESS, BITTERNESS, JEALOUSY
GREED, EGO, PRIDE, SHAMELESS,
LOW-SELFSTEEM 4FILLMENT,
FOCUS, AWARENESS, PRIDE,
JOY, LOVE, UNDERSTANDING, HAPPINESS
PERSISTENCE FAITH, GLORY, SPIRIT,
DIVINE, ESSENCE,
(IN THE POWER OF PRESENT)

Angel Ramos

❖ ❖ ❖

MAY YR EARS N YR EYES
THAT IN YR HEART,
MAY ENLIGHTEN YR PATH
THROUGH THIS JOURNEY
WE CALL UNDERSTANDING!

❖ ❖ ❖

PATH R CLEAR
BY UNDERSTANDING
THY SELF!!!!!

PAVE YOUR UNDERSTANDING
BY READING ITS PRESENT!!!!!

❖ ❖ ❖

IF WE CAN SEE N HEAR
THE WORD (WHY) IN DARKNESS,
WHY N I SAY
WHY CAN'T WE SEE
N HEAR IT ,
WHEN WE R IN
THE LIGHT A.K.A HAPPINESS
!!!!!!!!!!!!!!!! (SWEET-1) !!!!!!!!!!

❖ ❖ ❖

PATIENT IS A VIRTURE,
SO BECOME THE VIRTURE
 OF YR PATIENCE,,,,,,,,,,,,,,,,,
A GIFT OF PRESENT………..

✦ ✦ ✦

PRICE 4 THE IS
YR PRESENT.
SEE ALL THERE
THAT R PRESENT.

WORDS ! R SOOO BTFUL
IF U CAN SEE THERE PRESENTS…

✦ ✦ ✦

DAYS OR NIGHTS
DOES NOT MATTER,
WHAT MATTER
IS YR PRESENT

✦ ✦ ✦

LOVE?

SUCH A SIMPLE WORD
N COMPLEX
TOO SIMPLE
WHEN WE DEFINE

THE WORD
WITHIN OURSELF,
COMPLEX WHEN WE DON'T
.... CREATION,

✦ ✦ ✦

LIFE!!!! SUCH A STRONG WORD,
WHEN EMOTIONS TOUCH IT TURN VERY FRAGILE
,,,,,,,,,,,PERSISTENCE B YR PATH,,

✦ ✦ ✦

JUS CAUSE IT'S CLOUDI
RAININ, WINDY, N CHILI.
WE STILL HAVE THE RITE 2 DANCE ,
PARTY,LAUGH,SMILE,N ENJOY
THE DAY REGUARDLESS.
MAY THE JOY OF THE DAY
ENLIGHTEN YR EVENIN
,,,,,,,,,,,ALL NIGHT LONG

✦ ✦ ✦

SELF IS THE BULB!
N THINKS IS THE SWITCH,,,,,,,,,
PLEASE LIGHT THE BEAUTY OF EVERY
SMILE U PRESENT IN YR HEART!

✦ ✦ ✦

DONT LET THE RESPONSE OF THE SITUATION,
DEFINE THE THRUTH OF THE REALITY U TRULY (R)
,,,,,,,,,,,AWESOME,,,,,,,

A SECOND IS VALUABLE LIKE A DAY, 1 N ALL,,,,,,,,

✦ ✦ ✦

IT'S CRAZY !!
HOW (EASY) WE MAKE THE WORD
PAIN BURN A HOLE IN OUR HEART,
AND HOW (HARD) AND I MEAN HARD
THAT WE CAN'T MAKE THE WORD JOY
BLOSSOM IN OUR HEART,,,,,
TALK ABOUT SELF-fish.........................

✦ ✦ ✦

RECHARGIN THE BATTERY IN SELF READY SET PUFFSSSSSSS

✦ ✦ ✦

REFRESH YR BLESSIN WITH BTFUL THOUGHT!!

✦ ✦ ✦

SHINE YR LOVE WITH YR HEART,
N THE ESSENCE OF THE PRESENT WILL APEAR

,,,,,,,,,,,,,,,,,AKA SELF
SOUND CAN B VERY LOUD,
SOUND CAN B VERY QUIET,
ONLY WE CAN MAKE THAT HAPPEN
WITHOUT ANY SOUND?
!!!!!!!TRICKY AND DEFINING...............

✦ ✦ ✦

SUBSTANCE PRESENT IT SELF, IF WE CREATE IT.

✦ ✦ ✦

GRAVITY AINT NOTHING,
UNTIL THE HEART FeeL

✦ ✦ ✦

1 LITTLE SIMPLE TEAR
WEIGHT LIKE AN OCEAN,
IF WE DONT UNDERSTANDING
THE TRUE MEANING OF EMOTIONS
A.K.A PAIN!!
LOVE?
HOW COULD IT MEAN
EVERYTHING WITHOUT
A DEFINITON!
SELF BLESSIN

✦ ✦ ✦

IT'S SAD WHEN PEOPLE THINK .
THE SAYIN I HAVE NOTHIN TO SHOW 4 IT.
LITTLE BUT BIG THEY HAVE EVERYTHIN 2 SHOW 4 IT.
EVERYTHIN IS THEMSELF......
DO SELF-EXPLORATION N HAVE SELF 4FILLMENT,,,,,,,
NOTHIN N EVERYTHIN IS THE SAME
THEY JUS SIMPLE WORDS WITH DIFFERENce

✦ ✦ ✦

SAVE A LIVE,
N THE JOB IS VERY SIMPLE.
JUS SMILE N THE REST
WILL TALK 4 IT SELF,,,,,,,,,,,,,,,,,,,,,
THX 4 BEING U,,

✦ ✦ ✦

MAY THE DAY B THE GUIDANCE OF NIGHTS!!!!!!!!!!!!!!!!!!

THE WRATH OF THE STORM
IS NOTHING,
WHEN IT COME IT COME TO
THE BLESSIN OF THE WORDS,
WHICH IS EVERYTHIN,,,,,,,,,,,,,,
UNDERSTANDING,,,,,,

✦ ✦ ✦

GLORY, STRENGTH, SECURE, RESPONSIBLE,
FAITH, STRONG, WORTH, ARE, AM, I.
PUT ONE THESE WORD ON YR POCKET.
SO YR DAY MAY B EXPERIENCE.
MAY YR POCKET B YR HEART.

✦ ✦ ✦

BRIDGES R MADE FROM STEEL.
BUILDING R MADE BRICKS,
 BUT U ONLY (U) R MADE OUT OF LOVE!!!!,,,,,,,,,,,
SHARE IT N you B STRONGER

✦ ✦ ✦

WHY PAIN EMPTYS THE HEART,
WHEN IT OUR JOB 2 KEEP 4FILL,
PUT A BAND-AID CALL LOVE N IT WILL HEAL IT!!!!!!
 A THOUGHT THAT WE CALL FOOD
LOVE CONQUER THE WORLD, FAITH RULES IT.
MAY YR FAITH OF LOVE B YR WORLD,,,,,,,,,
BREEZE THE DAY CAUSE IT YR,,

✦ ✦ ✦

ONCE UPON A TIME
A CANDLE WAS LIT IN A DARK CAVE.
IN THE LIGHT EXPEREICE WAS CREATE.
IT SEEN BTFUL THING LIKE
LOVE, JOY, GLADNESS,
SECURENESS, REALITY,

BEST OF ALL LIFE.
WHEN THE CANDLE RAN OUT,
DARKNESS APEAR AGAIN.
THX 2 EXPERIENCE
THE CAVE WAS LIT,
IT LEARN 2 SHINE

✦ ✦ ✦

SEE WAT U CAN SEE,
FEEL WAT U CAN FEEL,
UNDERSTAND WAT U CAN UNDERSTAND.
THE TRUTH ABOUT THE CONCEPT OF SELF,,,,,,,,,,

✦ ✦ ✦

OUR FOOTPRINTS R OUR PAST,
OUR SHADOWS IS OUR FUTURE.
OUR UNDERSTANDIN IS OUR PRESENT OF
NOW,NOW,NOW,NOW,NOW,NOW,NOW!!!!!!!!!!!!!!!!!SWEET!!!!!!!

✦ ✦ ✦

HOW DO WE KNO THAT DIAMOND SHINE,
POLISH OURSELF 2 DAY,
N THE PRESENNT SHALL B BRIGHTEN,,,,,,

✦ ✦ ✦

HOW DO WE KNO THAT DIAMOND SHINE,

POLISH OURSELF 2 DAY,
N THE WEEKEND SHALL B BRIGHTEN,,,,,,

+ + +

IF U CAN HEAR THE LOVE
WHEN U LOVIN U (GOOD).
IF U CAN HEAR THE RESPECT
WHEN U RESPECTING U(AWESOME).
IF U CAB HEAR THE UNDERSTANDING
WHEN U UNDERSTANDING U (PERFECT)
,,,,,,,,,,,,,,,,,HEAR JUS BEING

+ + +

MYTH, THEORY, PUZZLE, ILLUTION, IMAGINATION, FICTION,
OR IS IT JUS THE REALITY................................SELF..........

+ + +

IT'S VERY HARD ,
N I MEAN VERY
2 LOVE.IF HUMAN EYES
THINK THAT THE SKIN POINT
 PRO:VERB AKA SELF,,,,,,
LOVE 1 ANOTHER

+ + +

MAKE SURE THAT WHEN WE GO IN2 THE CLOSET THIS MORNIN .
WE PUT SOMETHING THAT PRESENT OUR INNER BEING
LIKE LOVE JOY HAPPINESS GLADNESS.
N LET THE SMILE REPRESENT IT
BY YR AWARENESS THAT U FEEL AT THAT MOMENT
GUESS WAT IT ALWAYS WAS (U),,,,

✦ ✦ ✦

MAY THE PATTERN IN YR SOUL WEAVE LOVE
,,,,,,,,,,,,,,,,,,,,,,,,,,,,,,,,,,ENJOY THE SECOND

✦ ✦ ✦

SMOKE VANISHES N THE MIST,
EMOTIONS DISAPERE IN THE BLISS
............................QUEST 2 B DEFINE,,,

✦ ✦ ✦

WE FEEL TEARS WITH
PAIN, SHAME, GUILD, DISPAIR,
ETC, ETC, ETC .
WHEN R WE GOING 2 FELL THEM WITH
PLEASURE, JOY, 4FILMENT, STRENGHT,
ETC, ETC, ETC,,,,,,,,,,,,,,,,,,,,,,,,,,
SEEK 4 THE JOURNEY WE NEED

✦ ✦ ✦

THE GRASS IS GREENER IN THE OTHER SIDE ,
WHEN ADDING LOVE 2 IT,,,,,,,,,,,,,,,,,,
GROW SELF IT AWESOME,,

✦ ✦ ✦

only if u have the rite measurement!!!!
CAN SELF BE PRESENT…..

✦ ✦ ✦

MAY THE PRESENT REVEALTHE BEAUTY,
THAT WE POCESS!!REGUARDLESS

VIAGINIA FALL, NIAGRA FALL, N ANGEL FALL,
IF WE LOOK IN2 THEM THEIR ROAING NOISE,
VICIOUSS SOUND, POWERFUL CURRENTS.
JUS LIKE EMOTIONS.
GUESS WHAT IF WE LOOK AT THE
COMPLETE PICTURE THEY ALSO PRETTY   AWESOME.
WE CAN SEE BEAUTY THAT NEVER SEEN B4,,,,,,,,,
A.K.A (PRESENT) STORY TELLER

✦ ✦ ✦

MATTER IS MADE OF PARTICLE,
BECOME THE PARTICLE
THAT REALLY MATTER.
CAUSE ALL IN LIFE,
WE ALL MATTER…………….SELF

✦ ✦ ✦

PRESENT IS AWESOME IT BLESSES THE SOUL........

✦ ✦ ✦

UNDERSTANDING IS LIKE AN ENTITY,
THAT 4FIL THE SOUL,,,,,,,,,,,,,,,,
PRESENT ME ALL SECOND LONGGGGGGGGG

WORDS IS THE SOUND BOARD OF THE HEAR

✦ ✦ ✦

INTRODUCE SELF 2 SELF
DURING THE MOMENTS
 N EXPERIENCE THE EXPERIENCE.
====== I DARE U ==== ENJOY

✦ ✦ ✦

INTRODUCTIONS OF SELF IS THE EXPERIENCE 2 {B)

✦ ✦ ✦

THE MEETIN OF SELF
IS 2 KNOW 1 SELF..........

❖ ❖ ❖

SELF IS THE ONLY DESTROYER OF EMOTIONS..........

U CREATE SELF
U CREATE MEANING...............
U CREATE UNDERSTANDING
U CREATE THINKING............
BROUGHT TO YOU
BY A CUP OF WATER.........

❖ ❖ ❖

WHEN U MEET SELF
U MEET BLESSING.....

❖ ❖ ❖

THE ANSWER IS SELF,
THE QUESTION IS (U)!!!!
SELF,,,, INVENTORY,,,,,,,,,,,,

❖ ❖ ❖

CAN WE PUT 2GETHER THE QUESTION (WHY)
CAN WE SPELL THE WORD (WHY) CORRECTLY,,,,,,S-E-L-F

ABANDAMENT, IS 1 LACK OF UNDER-STANDING 1 SELF!!

Renaissance of Butterflies

✦ ✦ ✦

EMPTYNESS IS 2 SEE N NOT SEE,,,,,,,,,,,,,,,,,,,

✦ ✦ ✦

EVERYTHING IS RITE IN FRONT OF U
IF DONT OPEN YR EYE N SEE IT ,
RITE THERE.........

✦ ✦ ✦

THE MOUNTAIN IN YR BACK IS NOT THERE ,
ONLY THE GRAIN IN YR HAND....

✦ ✦ ✦

THIS ONLY 4 (u) THE 1 N ALL A.K.A SELF,,,,,,
MAY THE REACH OF YR HAND TOUCH THE PRESENT,
SO THE VISION OF YR EYE COULD SEE YR TRUE HEART!!!
MAY ALL HAVE A BTFUL SECOND !!!
RAIN OR SMILE OF EMOTION =ENJOY=

MAY THE ESSENCE B UPON (U)
IN YR DAILY PATH, 1 N ALL

✦ ✦ ✦

ESSENCE IS AWESOME

WHEN SEEN THE PRESENT,
YES IT CAN B DONE!!!!!!!!
SMILE N FEEL!!!!!!!!!!! WAA- LA

✦ ✦ ✦

A STONE CAN SPEAK,
IF A SELF TEACH SELF SLOWLY
N LISTEN 2 IT QUIETLY
2 THE SOUND OF THAT VOICE!!!!!!!!!!!

✦ ✦ ✦

IS IT EASY SAYIN!! I'VE (SWIM)THE HIGHEST MOUNTAIN,
OR I (CLIMB)THE LARGEST OCEAN,
OR I'M O.K. 2DAY WHEN WE KNOW WE NOT.
WHEN IT COME 2 LOVE, RESPECT, VALVE
THE UNDERSTANDING OF OUR SELF.
2 MAKE OUR PATH EASYEIR,
THAN WE CAN (SWIN) N (CLIMB) EASY!!!!!! THE POWER
MYTHOLOGY A.K.A TRUTH,
THEOLOGY A.K.A REALITY,
PHILOSOPHY A.K.A LIFE.
UNDERSTANDING THY SELF
CAN LIFT THE (FOG)
THE OVER THE HERIZON
A.K.A SELF!!!!!

✦ ✦ ✦

THE REALITY OF TRUTH IS (U).

(U) R THE TRUTH,
N (U) R THE REALITY OF THE PRESENT,
ANY PRESENT.
IT IS SAD THAT WE DONT SEE THE PRESENT IN THAT,
 ALWAYS WORRY ABOUT THING.
WHEN IT COME 2 THE PRESENT IT GIVE (U)
THE TRUTH N THE REALITY................
MIRACLE BEING IN WORDS

✦ ✦ ✦

ATSENTEE IS THE PRESENT OF DARKNESS B AWARE//////////
PRESENT IS THE LIGHT!!!!!!!!!

✦ ✦ ✦

FEEL WHAT'S THERE N IS UNSEEN,
AT THE PRESENT MOMENT (U) A.K.A
,,,,,,,,,,,,,,,,,,,SELF,,,,,,,,,,,,B----IT
CARING IS SEEING
THE SURROUNDIN THAT VIEW ALL
WHAT VIEW ALL IS SELF
,,,,,,,,,EASY IS CARING,,,,,,,,,

✦ ✦ ✦

THE WORLD IS SEEIN YR HEART,
N UNDERSTAND THE (WORDS) THAT U,
YES THAT U.PLACE THERE 2 BECOME IT,,,,,

NOTHING IS EVERYTHING WHEN SEEN,
EVERYTHING IS NOTHING WHEN SEEN
==== A.K.A BODY N SOUL.....

✦ ✦ ✦

THE PRE-4-MENCE THAT WE CREATE
THAT SEEN WITH IN OURSELF
,IS THE BLESSIN WE GIVE,,,,,,,,,

✦ ✦ ✦

MAGIC IS DONE , WITH A HAT, OR WAND.
N SOME R DONE WITH THE HEART!!!!!!

✦ ✦ ✦

thank U OH LORD 4 THE JOY OF TEAR
THAT AM FEEL AT THE PRESENT MOMENTS OF LIFE.
THOSE WORDS THAT U HAVE GIVING 2 ME
SO I CAN PRESENT THEN WITHIN MYSELF
 2 WENT IS NEEDED NOT WANTED
BLESS B THE PRESENT OF WORD
2 GUIDE SO WE CAN SEE
THE PATH OF JOY THAT IS I AM......

♦ ♦ ♦

SHEEP OR WOLF,
LIGHT OR DARK,
YES OR NO,
GOOD OR BAD,
DAY OR NIGHT,
POSITIVE OR NEGITIVE,
SIMPLE OR COMPLEX.
LITTLE WORDS WITH BIG DAMAGE,
WHY WE GIVE SO MUCH POWER
2 THESE WORDS.
EMOTIONS IS THE SOURCE
OF THAT POWER.
PLEASE B THE POWER OF WORDS
===WORDS OF THE SECOND===

♦ ♦ ♦

WHY DID WE CLIMD THE MOUNTAIN,
CAUSE IT'S THERE.
WHY DID WE SWAM THE OCEAN,
CAUSE IT'S THERE.
WHY DID WE NEED 2 ANSWER
THE WORDS (WHY),
CAUSE,THERE I AM..

♦ ♦ ♦

LOVE, RESPECT, VALUE
those 3 will secure

Angel Ramos

u,n u find the power
u lookin.which is littie o u.
hear them n experiece,
they r btful 2 listen in self .
u r the carrier of WORDS!!!!!!!!!!
carry them in yr HEART

✦ ✦ ✦

JOY IS CREATED BY THE UNDERSTANDING OF SELF.
N 2 THE TRUTH OF IT'S UNDERSTANDING,,,,,,,,

✦ ✦ ✦

2 B COMPLETE 1 MUST {PART}.
THIS IS NO YINK OR YANK,
THIS IS THE TRUTH 2 COMPLETE!!!!!
DIVERSION OF ILLUSIONS.
it would b the down of ourself if we dont,
get the word sometime out the picture
it our duty 2 conquer self solution of life
2 live a peace the way the words were ment 2 b..
remind yr self of 3 word
,love respect ,n value
foundation 4 security in self
understanding fight it .it's all (U)

✦ ✦ ✦

DONT LET YR APPERIENCE
DEFINE WHO U R.

LET THE BLESSIN DO THAT JOB .
IT IS IT,S DUTY 2 DO THAT.
MAY U FIND THE BLESSIN!!!!

✦ ✦ ✦

MATCHES, MAY B USE 2 LIGHT
THE PATH OF LIFE.
SOME FLAME LAST LONG,
SOME FLAME LAST SHORT.
THE SHORT ONES WERE TURN OFF
BY THE WIND OF EMOTIONS.
THE LONG ONE WERE PROTECTED
 BY THE UNDERSTANDING OF THE (HEART)

✦ ✦ ✦

A BOXER ASK, THE COACH.
THE DIFFERENT ABOUT HATE N LOVE.
THE COACH SAY .
WHEN U JAB AT SOMEBODY THAT'S (HATE).
N U HUG ANYBODY N I MEAN ANYBODY,
HOW THAT'S IS TRUE (LOVE)..................
LOVE N HATE, THE CONCEPT OF UNDERSTANDING.......

✦ ✦ ✦

IDOLIZATION ::::
PEOPLE LOVE 2 IDOLIZE
 MANY THING IN THE WORLD.
WHEN R WE GONNA IDOLIZE

THE TRUE GIFT THAT ALWAYS THERE,
GONNA B THERE REGUARDLESS.
THE WORD IDOL
START IN A TINY
PLACE IN THE HEART.
KEEP IDOLIZING IT,
WILL BECOME A COMPLETE HEART,
THAT THE TRUTH
A WORD IS TINY IN NOTHING
BUT IT FILLS A UNIVERSE

✦ ✦ ✦

THE MEANING 2 PERSONAL GROWTH IS 2 SEE..........................
.........WATCH IT!!!!
GOVERMENT, RELIGION, FAMILY, SELF-HELP
WHO REALLY IN REALITY IS INCHARGE
OR IN CONTROL ON UNDERSTANDING THY SELF.
REALLY WHO,WHO,WHO,THEY R OR (U) R...........
THIS IS A MOMENT OF THE AWAKENNING OF CONTROLL
OR IN CHARGE OF SELF.........

✦ ✦ ✦

PRESENT IS ALWAY'S THERE NO MATTER
WHAT FLAVOR. THE REAL MATTER IS R (U) THERE....
------- careful slippery road on the one ----------------

✦ ✦ ✦

1 ST WAR EVER ::

THE WAR OF SELF,
THE WAR OF BROTHER,
THE WAR OF COUNTRIES,
THE WAR OF THE WORLD,
ALL WERE SIMPLE N RESOLVE,
EXPECT THE COMPLEX
WAR OF THEM ALL.
THE WAR OF SELF,
THE PEACE TREADY 4 THIS WAR
 START WITH LOVE THY SELF,
RESPECT THY SELF,
VALUE THY SELF…
DAYS R MADE BY THINKING,
AS TIME IS PRESENT EVERY SECOND.
SO PRESENT THE TIME
SO (U) CAN MAKE YR DAY.
THE UNDERSTANDING OF THE THINKIN
GIVE (U) THE PRESENT THAT (U) R
,,,,,,,,,,BTFUL,BRILLAINT,N WORTHY,,,,,

✦ ✦ ✦

SOFTLY, EXPERIENCE YR THINKING.
LIVE IN IT 4 A WHILE,
ASK YR SELF WAT R THE RESULT
I BET U HAVE AN ANSWER.
N THE ANSWER IS UNDERSTANDING.............
DIVINE, ESSENCE, SPIRIT,
GIFT LIFE, N MIRACLE,
NEED I SAY MORE ,,, SECOND THE WORDS

Angel Ramos

✦ ✦ ✦

SAYING OF THE UNDERSTANDING,
LIGHT THE PATH OF PEOPLE JOURNEY.
MAY THE JOURNEY THAT U SEEK,
LIGHT THE PATH THAT U R,,,,,,,,,,,,,,
SEEK, DESTROY, CONQUER,
BECOME EVERYTHING IN SELF…..
NOW!!!! IS THE POWER OF THE PRESENT,
THAT GIVE (U) THE ABILITY…………..2,,,,,,,,,,,,,,,,B,,,

✦ ✦ ✦

NOW!!! IS THE WHEN N WHERE
THAT U SEE.AT THE MOMENT
THE TRUTH PRESENT ITSELF.
AT THE MOMENT THE ABILITY
APEAR 2 PERFORCE IT DUTY
!!!! KEEPIN FOCUS……….

✦ ✦ ✦

ONCE UPON A TIME
(DARKNESS)LACK OF UNDERSTANDING THY SELF
UNDERSTANDING THY SELF(LIGHT)
……………THE END
………THE TIME OF HISTORY………..

✦ ✦ ✦

SINCE, THE PAST WE ALWAYS
LOOK 4 OUR DESTINY.
WE ALWAYS KNOWN
THAT OUR DESTINY IS IN THE FUTURE.
GUESS WAT THE DESTINY
ALWAYS BEEN THE (PRESENT)
SINCE THE BEGINNING OF TIME....................

4 (1 SELF) 2 LOOK THERE, 2 (1 SELF) MUST SEE HERE!!!!

✦ ✦ ✦

THE TRUTH IN ALL REALITY IN LIFE.
IS 2 ENJOY THE EXPERIENCE OF THE MOMENT,
IN THE PRESENT OF THE BEING.....

✦ ✦ ✦

FEELIN THE AIR
IN THE BOTTLE,
IS LIKE SEEING
THE ESSENCE
IN THE BODY ,,,,,,,,,,,,,,,,
TRUE MEANNIN
OF ENLIGHTMENT,,,,,,,,,,,,

✦ ✦ ✦

AN EMPTY GLASS
WITHOUT WATER,

Angel Ramos

IS LIKE A BODY
WITHOUT A SPIRIT.
SO FILL THE EMPTY
GLASS WITH THE SPIRIT...

✦ ✦ ✦

WHEN WE SEE OUR (PATH),
WE SEE PAIN.
WHEN R WE GOIN
2 SEE JOY IN OUR (PATH).......
LET'S MAKE A CLEAN SWEEP

✦ ✦ ✦

THE WORLD IS YR,
THE 1ST STEP WITH YR HEART.
NOT WITH YR LEGS.

✦ ✦ ✦

E-Z DOES WONDER,
PATIENCE EXPERIENCE LIFE....

✦ ✦ ✦

LOVE CLEAR THE MIND.
RESPECT CLEAR THE HEART.
N VALUE CLEAR THE PRESENT......................

✦ ✦ ✦

MAY THE TRUTH BE
THE LOVE THAT
U FEEL 4 SELF.
THE RESPECT THAT
U FEEL 4 SELF.
THE VALUE THAT
U FEEL 4 SELF.
MAY THESE THREE WORDS
B PLANTED IN
THE BEST SOIL
THAT LIFE IS AFFORDING.
IN A LITTLE
PLACE IN THE SELF
CALLED THE (HEART),,,,,,,,
BLESSIN CONQUER DREAMS,,,

✦ ✦ ✦

ONE LESS IS MORE THAN......................
................................POWER OF WORDS
ILLUSIONS SAYS
THERE R MANY PATH,
THE WORDS SAY
THERE IS ONLY ONE,,,,,,,
.... UNDERSTANDIN ,,,,

✦ ✦ ✦

CREATION START WITH A LETTER,

BELIEVING START WITH AN (HONEST) WORD!!!!

✦ ✦ ✦

1 IS 2 MANY, AS MANY IS 2 1.
THE UNITY OF THE WORDS WITH IN 1SELF,,,,,

✦ ✦ ✦

2 GROW ONE MUST DECREASE, 2 DECREASE ONE MUST GROW,,, THE BIRTH OF WORDS,,,,

✦ ✦ ✦

PEOPLE WALK ON DREAM,
PEOPLE WALK ON FICTION,
PEOPLE WALK ON AIR.
IT BETTER 2 SEE OUR PATH,
IF WE WALK ON THE GROUND
......AWARENESS 2 PEOPLE PATH

✦ ✦ ✦

CANVAS IS MADE 4 PAINTIN,
WE PAINT SAD THING N BTFUL THING.
PAPER IS MADE 4 WRITTEN,
WE WRITE SAD THING N BTFUL THING.
LIFE IS MADE 4 LIVING,
WE LIVE SAD THING N BTFUL THING.

WE NEED 2 LIVE THE BTFUL THING,
NOT WANT THE SAD THING.
(WRITE) THE CANVAS, (PAINT) THE   PAPER

✦ ✦ ✦

THE SPIRIT OF 1, IS THE BONDIN OF OTHERS!!!!!!

✦ ✦ ✦

SIMPLE!!!!! UNDERSTANDIN EASY PLEASURE
THE LIFE OF BTFUL TRUE BEING
IN THE PRESENT OF THY ONE,,,,,,,,,,
PRESENTS IS (U),,,,

✦ ✦ ✦

COMPLEX BRING THE PAST,
SIMPLE BRING THE FUTURE.
N THE PRESENT BRING THE BEAUTY
OF JUS BEIN TRUE SELF,,,,,,,,,,,,,,
SOFT N STRONG,,,,,,,,,,,,,,,,,,,,

✦ ✦ ✦

SELF SAID I'LL WALK
WITH AM EVEN IN THE RAIN,,,,,,,,,,,,,,,,,,
UNDERSTANDIN THE PROTECTION

✦ ✦ ✦

B JUS 2 START...

✦ ✦ ✦

OUR NAME DOESN'T DEFINE WHO WE R,
OUR HEART DOES..... (AM)

WHAT IS THE REAL WAY 2 (4 GIVE).
FEED YR SELF EMOTIONS,
OR FEED YR SELF UNDERSTANDIN
,,,,4 GIVING IS A ROSE THAT GROW,,,,,

✦ ✦ ✦

A LOT OF CHARACTERS,
1 SYLLaBLE,,,,,,,,,,,,,,,,,,,,,ALL

✦ ✦ ✦

KNOWING IS KNOWLEDGE, UNDERSTANDIN IS LIVING
MUST I DRAW A PICTURE........

✦ ✦ ✦

HAPPINESS IS IN THE LIGHT,
THE SWITCH CALL THE SMILE
 IS NEXT 2 THE HEART.
N IT TURN ON BY UNDERSTANDING,,,,,,,,

✦ ✦ ✦

PAIN? CAN B COLD OR IT CAN B HOT.
JOY? CAN B COLD OR IT CAN B JOY.
SELF? CAN B PAIN OR CAN B JOY
,,,,,CAN B SIMPLY OR CAN B COMPLEX,,,,,

WOW? 2 REALIZE (U) WILL ALWAYS B THERE ,, WOW!!!!!..........SELF.......

✦ ✦ ✦

BEAUTY, IS WAT (U) GIVE N EXPRESS.
GIVE IT 2 SELF N THE PRESENT WILL (B)........

✦ ✦ ✦

ASK? YR SELF DO I REALLY WALK
WHEN I (SEE). PICTURE
COVERING YR EYE
CAN (U) REALLY WALK.
(C) WE NEED OUR HEART
2 WALK TRUELY, NOT OUR EYES,,,,,,,,,
THE HEART IS THE LIGHT
OF THE PATH 2 SEE !!!!!!!!!!

✦ ✦ ✦

HOW MANY ELEPHANT

FIT INSIDE A PEANUTBUTTER JAR.
1 IF U UNDERSTANDING, MANY IF U THINK........
ONCE UPON A TIME I LEARN,
2 DAY I TEACH -THE END-------------
LONG STORY SHORT VERSION!!!

✦ ✦ ✦

SEE THE SILENT OF THE HEART,
SO U CAN HEAR THE LIGHT

✦ ✦ ✦

FRIENDSHIP IS IN THE HEART, NOT IN THE VISION,,,

✦ ✦ ✦

FRIENDSHIP, IS LIKE A PENNY IN THE POCKET.
THEY WOULD KISS YR ASS 2 TAKE IT,
THEN THEY PLAY CUPID WHEN COMFRONT ABOUT IT..............
IM GLAD ON NEXT 2 THA HEART
UNDERSTANDING 2 THINKING..................

✦ ✦ ✦

CRUCIFIX IS LIKE WALKIN IN DARKNESS, THINK SO THE LIGHT GOOOO ON!!!!

✦ ✦ ✦

IF THERE R 18 PEOPLE IN A RM..,
HOW MANY SOUL R THERE,,,,,,,,,,,,,,,
ANS?,,,,1 N ALL THE SAME,,,

✦ ✦ ✦

FUSTRATION (R) EMOTION.
LOVE, RESPECT, VALUE
MIX THEM 2GETHER
N (U) HAVE THE ANTI-DOPE
4 LIFE 2 B,,,,,,

✦ ✦ ✦

LOVE IS A TRADITION, NOT A MISSION

✦ ✦ ✦

CHANGE YR CONSCIOUS 2 ESSENCE,
BY FEELIN THE BLACK SMOKE
N CHANGE IT 2 WHITE SMOKE.
ITS CALLED AN ILLUSIONS
BUT IT WORK IF U BELIEVE
IN THE (WORDS), NOT THE ILLUSIONS

✦ ✦ ✦

Angel Ramos

A DECISION WITHIN THE THOUGHT, IS A ACTION WITHIN THE (WILL).

✦ ✦ ✦

PEOPLE GOT THE (GIFT) 4 GAP,
ASK SELF DO WE HAVE THE GAP 4 THE (GIFT),,,,,
UNDERTSANDING ASKING THINKING
DO YOU KNOW, what YOU ASKING YOUR SELF

✦ ✦ ✦

IF U WERE ON TOP OF A MOUNTAIN
U WOULD WALK DOWN 2 GET HERE.
IF U WERE ON THE OTHER SIDE OF THE OCEAN
 U WOULD SWIM 2 B HERE.
THE UNDERSTANDING OF HERE
 IS NOT THAT FAR IT RITE THERE
!!!!!!!!!!SELF!!!!!!!---------HERE IS BLESSIN....

✦ ✦ ✦

LIFE IS A TREASURE LETS POLISH WHILE IT STILL HERE!!!!!!!!!!!! MAY THE GONE B REMEMBER,,,,,,,,,,,,,,,,,,,,,,,,,,,,,, BLESSIN 2 THE UNDERSTANDING,,,,,,,

✦ ✦ ✦

LIFE SAY!!! THINKING IS NOT THE WAY, UNDERSTANDING IS.
IN REALITY THAT'S WHAT THINKING IS REALLY ALLLLLLL
(ABOUT)
.,,,,,,,,,,SO THINK,

✦ ✦ ✦

UNDERSTANDING IN LIFE CAN B TAKEN,
N LEAVE A VIOD IN US.
THE BEST WAY 2 FILL THE VIOD
IS 2 REMEMBER
WHAT WAS TAKEN FROM US
,A.K.A THE MOMENT,,,,,,,,,,,

✦ ✦ ✦

THERE A NEED 2 LOOK ,
WHERE (U) NEED 2 LOOK!!!!!
UNDERSTANDING COUNSELING thinking........
LEFT IS WAT IS FOUND THE WORDS!!!!!
THAT B SIMPLE....................

✦ ✦ ✦

WORDS R PERFECTS THE WAY self MADE THEN, WHY PLAY WITH THEM!!!!!
A TEACHING OF UNDERTANDING TO THINKING

✦ ✦ ✦

A WORLD IS EVERYTHIN
THATSHOULD NOT B AWAY
FROM ANYBODY ,
SO GIVE THAT WORLD
2 YR SELF.
N DONT TAKE IT AWAY,,,,,,,,,,,,,

✦ ✦ ✦

ts rite there in from of self look at the mirror that inside of (U),
look at the words love, respect, n valve, more that (U) R
GIFT COME IN DIAMOND,
GOLD, CARS, HOUSES, BOATS,
BRACELET, CARDS, ETC,ETC.
HAVE ANYBODY EVER FIND
THE GIVE OF UNDERSTANDING,,,,,,,,,,,,,,,,,,,,,,
FREE AT CHARGE
NO BATTERIES INCLUD,,,,,,,,,,,,,

✦ ✦ ✦

STATEMENT N COMMENT
R LIKE OPINION,
THEY BOTH SUCK TISSUE
R USE AFTER EACH ONE.
UNDERSTANDIN IS THE
TRUE HONEST BASE.
4 THE TRUE WORDS WHAT
DEFINE REALITY, LIFE, TRUTH,
2 THE reasons OF JOY IN THIS (WORLD).....

✦ ✦ ✦

THE BASE IN OUR HEART ,
IS THE SOLID FUNDATION
OF THE UNDERSTANDIN,,,,,,,,,,,
((((WORDS)))) N SEAL WITH YR KISS
JUS LIKE STAR
LIGHT THE UNIVERSE,
((WORDS)) LIGHT
THE PATH 2 THY SELF,,,,,,,,
THE BLESS OF ALL
IS 1 SIMPLE WORD,,,,,,,

✦ ✦ ✦

STAR SHINE, MOON BRIGHTEN,
N HEART ENLIGHTEN,,,,,,,,,,,,,,,,,,,,,,,,,
BECOME THE QUEST OF THE JOURNEY
THAT ((U)) TRULY SEEK,,,,,,,,,,,,,

✦ ✦ ✦

BOUNDARIES CAN B
ENLIGHTEN IN ANYBODY,
N I MEAN ANYBODY PATH,,,,,,,,,
USE THINKIN AS YR LANTEN
AS WE TAKE THE STEPS!!!1

✦ ✦ ✦

MAY THE PATH THY WALK 2 DAY ,
B THE REPERSENTATION OF THY HEART.
................PEACE B YR LIGHT..

LIFE IS A PIECE OF CAKE, ALL (U) NEEDS IS THE RITE INGRIGIENT!!!

♦ ♦ ♦

THE BODY OF WAR WITHIN 1SELF,
IS CAUSE BY THE LACK OF UNDERSTANDIN
1 HAS OF THEMSELVES,,,,,,,,,,
FAMOUS QUOTE IS (((-UNDERSTAND-THY-SELF-)))
VERY APPRECIATED IF LEARN
2 LISTEN N LISTEN 2 LISTEN----THY SELF,,,,

♦ ♦ ♦

ANTI-VENOM 4 DEPRESSION IS LOVE (((SIMPLE))),,,,,,,,,,BELIEVE!!!

♦ ♦ ♦

THE POrTIONS OF LOVE IS THE BIGGINNIG OF THE LOVING ((-HEART-)) NEED WATER GET A CUP SIMPLE, NEED (thinking) THE WORD UNDERSTANDIN!!!!!!!!

✦ ✦ ✦

2 NIGHT 4 DESSERT IS LOVE THY SELF,
RESPECT THY SELF, VALUE THY SELF,,,,,,,,,,
VITAMIN 4 THE (((((((((HEART)))))))

✦ ✦ ✦

WAT IS A PLACE
SIMPLE IS SPACE.
LOOK AT THE WORD
N FEEL U SHELL BECOME AS IS.
NOW 4 FILL THAT SPACE WITH WORD
N U SHALL BECOME I AM..........

✦ ✦ ✦

UNDERSTANING IS simplex,
THINKING IS complex,
N BEING IS PERPLEX...............
BELIEVE,,,,N,,,,,EASE

✦ ✦ ✦

THINKING IS UNDERSTANDING,
UNDERSTANDING IS LIVING, N LIVING IS SELF..........................
........................WHICH IS ALL IN ((1))
LISTENING 2 THE TREES THAT
FALL FAR DEEP IN2 THE FORREST.
IT LIKE LISTENNING 2 THE WORDS

THAT R REAL CLOSE 2 THE HEART .
THE SHAME IS THAT U DONT HEAR
THEM OR SEE THEM. WOW
HOW FAR R WE FROM OURSELF
........JUS A POINT 2 VIEW........................

✦ ✦ ✦

FAR IS NOT NEAR,
IT'S RITE THERE........

✦ ✦ ✦

NEAR IS NOT FAR,
IT'S RITE THERE......

✦ ✦ ✦

PERTAINING 2 SELF,
NOT A FICTION IS A REALITY
THAT WE MUST MAINTAIN
REGARDLESS THAT CIRCUMSTANCE
THAT APPEARS AT OUR PRESENTS MOMENTS...

THINKING IS UNDERSTANDING,
UNDERSTANDING IS LIVING,
N LIVING IS SELF..................
WHICH IS ALL IN ((1))

✦ ✦ ✦

mTHINKING IS UNDERSTANDING, UNDERSTANDING IS LIVING, N LIVING IS SELF..WHICH IS ALL IN ((1))

✦ ✦ ✦

AS THE REC..... SAYS --DON'T FIGHT THE FEELIN—
A.K.A EMOTIONS R LIKE WAVE SOONER OR LATER
THEY WILL DRIED UP WITHOUT THE MOP OR TOWELS,,,,,,,,,,
UNDERSTANDING IS THE BEST WAY 2 DRY OUR TEARS!!!!

✦ ✦ ✦

GAIN IS 2 B SELF,,,,,,,,,,,,,,,,,,,,,,,,,, SIMPLEX B, COMPLEX SELF

✦ ✦ ✦

SEARCH IS AN AVENTURE
THAT IS THE JOURNEY
2 ENLIGHTMENT IN THE reason
OF DEFINNING (((WHAT IS)))...
CASUALTY R PEOPLE
WITH EMOTIONAL
INFLUENCING SELF,
LOVE, RESPECT, VALUE SELF
R 3 PAIN KILLER.

✦ ✦ ✦

A LIGHT CAN BURN (U),
A LIGHT CAN SAVE (U)....
THE MEANING OF
DEFINITION OF DEFINNING,,,,,,,,,,,,,,,,,,,
SEE THE TRUE LIGHT,,,,,

✦ ✦ ✦

MAY THAT MELODY
 B YR SMILE
SO IT GUIDE U
DURING YR PATH,,,,,,,,,,,,,
MELODY R ENLIGHTMENTS

✦ ✦ ✦

THE PROPOSITION WAS MADE
THOSE WHO BELIEVE
IN THE WORDS
SHALL B THE LIGHT!!!!!!,,,,
ANGEL HIDES IN THE BLISS
OF THE SOULS,
WORDS LIGHT THEIR PATH
SO THEY CAN B SEEN
,,,,,,,,,,,,,,,,,,,,,,,,,,,SELF,,

✦ ✦ ✦

PRESENT APPEAR UPON THE ESSENCE IN LIFE,
CHOOSE A WORD WITH YR HEART
N THAT IS THE ESSENCE OF AN (SELF).................

APPEARS IN WORDS CONQUER IN HEART.........

✦ ✦ ✦

JOY IS SIMPLE,
JOY IS FREE,
JOY IS (U).
SOOOO ENJOY
YR DAYS........

✦ ✦ ✦

CAVE-IN R CUASES OR DEPRESSION,
LOVE IS THE LIGHT OF THE CAVE........................
SPIKE A LIGHT IN THE CAVE OF YR LIFE!!!!
PROGRESS IS SUCCESS,
SUCCESS IS 1SELF.......................
B THE SUCCESS OF YR PURE SELF.........

✦ ✦ ✦

BEGINNING IS NOT
THE END OF NOTHING,
THE END IS NOT
THE BEGINNING OF EVERYTHING..........

✦ ✦ ✦

HOW CAN A MILE B SO FAR,
WHEN U ALREADY TOOK THE 1ST STEP!!!

❖ ❖ ❖

B 4 WE SEE THE FORREST,
WE MUST TAKE OUT THE SPLINTER
FROM OUR EYES.
THAT WE CREATED IN 2 A TREE!!

❖ ❖ ❖

UNDERSTANDING IS THE CREATER
OF WORDS THAT U NEED 2 BECOME!!!...
the different between
NOTHING n EVERYTHING
is SOMETHING!!!

❖ ❖ ❖

AN AWESOME GEM IS A WORDS
THAT MAKES THE HEART SHINE......

❖ ❖ ❖

1 TOO!! COLOR THE WORLD
4 WAT IS TRULLY IS,
1 MUST USE THE BRUSH
THAT IS THE HEART!!!

❖ ❖ ❖

THE SMILE IS OUT OF PLACE,

CAUSE THE HEART IS NOT IN IT PLACE!!!

✦ ✦ ✦

SENDIN HEART 2 THOSE of KNO,
N DONT KNO COMPLETEY TH SUM......

✦ ✦ ✦

LOVE WALK WITH U IF U STEP RITE..

WHY WE DWELL ON OUR
EMOTIONS LIKE CRAZY,
WHEN WE OURSELF TRIGGER THEM
N POINT FINGER 2 OTHER,
BUT NEVER SPENT 1 SEC...
ON OUR HEART!!!!

✦ ✦ ✦

EXPIRIENCING YR EYES
AS THE PRESENT
TALKS WITHIN THY HEARTS.
IT A BLESSIN THAT SHOULD
TAKEN CARE OFF,,,,,,,,,,,,
>WORDS< MAKES DIFFERENTS........

✦ ✦ ✦

JOURNEY R
MADE BY DECICIONS,
NOT BY DREAMS

♦ ♦ ♦

SEE WHAT U CAN SEE,
FEEL WHAT U CAN FEEL,
TOUCH WHAT U CAN TOUCH....................
THE CORE OF THE HEART!!

THE GIVENESS OF HAPPINESS,
IS THE UNDERSTANDING PLEASURE 2 > B <.....

♦ ♦ ♦

SPACE 4 RENT!!!!!!!!!!!!!!..............SELF...

♦ ♦ ♦

STEP R FIRST 2
ENLIGHTEN YR PATH,
NOT 2 WALK!!!!!!!!!!!!!!!...............
IF U WALK IN SiLENCE
U WALK IN WATER..........

♦ ♦ ♦

A PARTICLE OF
UNDERSTANDING CAN STOP,

WAVES OF EMOTIONS.
CAUSE WKEDS R FULL OF
 PARTICLE OF EMOTIONS,
THAT CAN MESS
THE WAVES OF UNDERSTANDING.................
GUARD IS THE KEY, LOVE IS THE SHEILD........

✦ ✦ ✦

LOVE CLEAR THY PATHS,
AS EMOTIONS COVERS IT!!!!!!!!!!!!!!!!........
.SIMPLE.....SELF
WHY U MADE ME 2 LOVE,
UNDERSTAND, N BELIEVE.
N I MADE MYSELF 2 POINT FINGERS,
2 BITTER MYSELF,
N MADE MYSELF SELF-FISH
BY NOT BELIEVING IN MYSELF
...................I-AM= I-AM.

✦ ✦ ✦

SUN BRIGHT, HEARTS SMILE, N present BLESS,
WORDS THAT R CONTAIN ON THE WHOLE DAYS.
MANDATORY MUST CARRY THESE WORDS
ON THE PRESENTS OF THE PATH!!!!!!!!

✦ ✦ ✦

BECOME THE DAY N SHINE!!!!!!!!
BECOME THE MOMENT N BE..........

Angel Ramos

BECOME THE SELF N AM
BECOME THE SECOND N PRESENT

✦ ✦ ✦

WHAT MATTER IS
WHAT U DO WITH TIME,
DON'T LET THE MATTER
OF TIME DO U.......

NO MATTER WHERE
U STAND IN THE WORLD,
U R THE SAME.
NO MATTER WHERE
THEY GO AROUND THE
WORLD THEY R
LIKE U THE SAME
SAME IS A SELF

✦ ✦ ✦

IF U CAN SEE ITS CALLED WATCHING,
IF U CAN LOVE ITS CALLED BLESSIN,
IF U CAN RESPECT ITS CALLED SHINE,
IF U CAN VALUE ITS CALLED THE PATH
..................SELF ON SELF

✦ ✦ ✦

LET THE LIGHT OF YR HEART
LIGHT YR PATH OF THE PRESENT

THAT NEEDS!!!!!!!!!

+ + +

PEACE B WALKED 2-DAY..

+ + +

IF U STAND STILL LOVE
EXPRESS IT SELF ALL OVER,
IMAGINE FEELIN IT,,,,,

+ + +

THE PAST CAN FIX THE FUTURE,
IF U UNDERSTAND THE PRESENT!!!!!!!!!!!

+ + +

IF U THINK A MILE
IS A LONG DISTANCE,
LOOK AT THE DISTANCE
U HAVE YR SELF FROM YR HEART!!!!!!!!!!
DISTANCE IS A DECISION..

+ + +

A WALK IS ONLY A STEP AWAY!!!,,,,,
A DECISION IS ONLY A <<THINK>> AWAY!!!!

Angel Ramos

✦ ✦ ✦

EXPERIENCE IS JUS A WORD!!
BUT IF U SEE WAT IT MEAN 2 1-SELF.
THE MEANNING OF THAT IS MORE
BTFUL THEN U CAN SEE,,,,,,,EXPERIENCE!!

ME!!!!!!!!! U??????????? US...............
N ALL.............BEING AS ONE

✦ ✦ ✦

2 WALK AS A BLESSIN
U MUST BECOME AS U R BTFUL...

✦ ✦ ✦

walkin THE DISTANCE
IS LOVIN YR SELF!!!!!!!!!!!

MOVEMENT OF ACTION✦ ✦ ✦

A BLANK CHECK HAS -- VALUE—
IF U LOVE YR SELF!!!!!!!!

✦ ✦ ✦

DAY'S CAN B FULL OF
---------VALUE------------
IF U 4 FILL THE SECONDS!!!!

✦ ✦ ✦

2 CATCH A DREAM,
1 MUST LOOK 4 EVERYTHIN
BY DOIN NOTHING!!!!...............
THINK IS THE QUEST 2 4FILL.

THE STRINGS OF ((WORDS)),
WHEN COMES 2
UNDERSTANDING THY ((WORDS)).
U CAN WEAVES BEAUTY IN 2 YR LIFE.
BY DEFINNING WAT TRUE ((WORDS))
 MEAN 2 THE UNDERSTANDIN 2 - B - !!!!!!!!

✦ ✦ ✦

2 CATCH A DREAM,
1 MUST LOOK 4 EVERYTHIN
BY DOIN NOTHING!!!!...............
THINK IS THE QUEST 2 4FILL.

✦ ✦ ✦

THE PROPHECY OF WORDS,
IS THE UNDERSTANDIN OF THE
SEEDS U PLANTS 2 DEFINE YR SELF
...............KNOW THY SELF....

✦ ✦ ✦

SOUND R BTFUL,
JUS LIKE WORDS WITH
THY UNDERSTANDIN!
LISTEN TO VIEW..........
VISION HARMONY................
THE ILLUSION OF WORDS,
IS THE ROUGHNESS WE DISPLAY
THEM WHEN NOT SEEN!!!

♦ ♦ ♦

seeing the words with yr heart,
n hearing the words with yr eyes.
GIVE THE MEANNING OF UNDERSTANDIN.
UNDERSTANDING OPENS A HERIZON
THAT R EXPRESS AS BLESSIN!!!!!

♦ ♦ ♦

I AM WHICH PICTURE
Said the present of words

♦ ♦ ♦

SEE U SHALL B SEEN,
WALK N U SHALL WALK,
BELIEVE N U WILL BELIEVE!!!!
..........BELIEVER BELIEVE...

♦ ♦ ♦

BONDING IS THE SMILE B-4 BONDING
CARVE A BLESS DAY…………..

SOUND IS LIKE MUSIC,
IT GIVE POWER AT
THOSE MOMENTS WE HEAR,
SO HEAR THE SOUND
THAT R IN YR HEART IS
THE MUSIC OF LIFE.
SO HERE YR LIFE 2-DAY!!!!!!

✦ ✦ ✦

OCEAN R TEARS, MADE OUT OF
MISUNDERSTANDING OF WORDS
 THAT WOULD DRIVE THE MIND INSANE
…………….LOVE IS THE TOWEL…

✦ ✦ ✦

WE Were THERE WHEN WE CRY!
WE Were THERE WHEN WE FELT BITTER.
WE Were THERE WHEN SADNESS WAS PRESENT
.,,,,,,,,,,, WE R US ,,,,,,,,,,,,,,THX U WE R US……….

✦ ✦ ✦

A PARTICLE OF DARKNESS,
CAN KILL THE WHOLE (LIGHT)….

Angel Ramos

✦ ✦ ✦

CLEARANCE UNCOVER DARKNESS....................SELF..
A PARTICLE CAN BECOME
A MOUNTAIN IF U LET IT RULE U......

✦ ✦ ✦

BECOME THE STRENGTH
THAT U R ,WHEN U BELIEVE....

✦ ✦ ✦

IF IT MOVING LEAVE IT ALONE,
IS ONLY AN EMOTIONS

✦ ✦ ✦

 AS POWERFUL AS YR SMILE
THE PRESENT LANTERNS

✦ ✦ ✦

U CAN MELT
ANY AVALANCE,
IF THE LOVE COME
FROM THE HEART!!!!!!!!

✦ ✦ ✦

FIRE WALKIN IS EASY JUS WALK
WITH A BUCKET OF LOVE!!!

THEY SAY THAT WE CAN'T COVER THE SKY,
CLOSE YR EYE N TELL ME........

✦ ✦ ✦

SIMPLE WILL GIVE U THE WORLD,
IF U BECOME EVERYTHIN

✦ ✦ ✦

A GOOD CRUSADER CONQUER
EVERYTHIN IN THEIR HEART
,,,,,,,,,, SO SAIL AWAY......

✦ ✦ ✦

IF U LEAVE IT ALONE,
IT WON'T FOLLOW!!!!!!!!!!!!
................EMOTIONS

✦ ✦ ✦

PUT THEM IN THE BACK,
DON'T LETS IT PRESENT ITSELF.
...................EMOTION

✦ ✦ ✦

IF U WALK STANDING STILL,
U THE ONE THAT'S AHEAD................
FOCUS OF THE LIGHT.....

A SEC..... IS A LIFE TIME,
ENJOY YR SEC....
AS IT PRESENT ITSELF..................
ENJOY YR SHINE 2-DAY....

✦ ✦ ✦

THE STRONG ONE IS THE ONE THAT THINK.
THE WEAK ONE IS THE ONE THAT THINK...................A.K.A SELF

✦ ✦ ✦

DURING THE DAYS PUT
SOME SEC IN YR HEART.
WHO KNOW A THAT SEC
YOU JUST LOVE YR SELF.......

✦ ✦ ✦

ESSENCE GIVE U THE OPPORTUNITY TO LIVE.
DIVINE GIVE U THE OPPORTUNITY TO LOVE.
WILL GIVE U THE OPPORTUNITY TO BE!!!!

✦ ✦ ✦

make yr day a blessin,
so u can sleep in comfort
...................lastin joy...........

THE ACTIONS COME
FROM THE HEART,
AFTER THE UNDERSTANDIN...............
B-4 ITS PRESENTATION

✦ ✦ ✦

BEAUTYS R THE TEAR
THAT GIVE US
STRENGHT 2 STAND...........
WOW IS THE WILL

✦ ✦ ✦

u could change a ROCK in-2 solid WATER
..............................SELF PLANNIN

✦ ✦ ✦

STEP MAKES PEOPLE FALL,
UNDERSTANDIN MAKES PEOPLE LOVE
......................BIRTH OF REBIRTH

✦ ✦ ✦

REFORMATION, IS THE UNDERSTANDIN OF THE CREATER

........WORDS THAT WALK..

✦ ✦ ✦

B-4 BUILDIN 1 MUST HAVE THE RITE WORDS IN THERE PLACE...............GROWTH..

CLIMB, REACH, WALK, STEP,
NO MATTER WAT WORDS U CHOOSE
COMPLETE YR DAY WITH JOY...

✦ ✦ ✦

4-FILLMENT R DAY FILL
WITH U CALLED BLESSIN......

✦ ✦ ✦

GLORY, N BLESSIN,
R DEFINE AS U
SMILE IN THE MOMENTS!!!!!!!!!!!!!!!!!!!!!...
IT CALLED THE HEART THAT READ...

✦ ✦ ✦

sound could come in tear,
also sound could come in smile......

✦ ✦ ✦

a logo is like a heart,
u can represent love....

✦ ✦ ✦

WHY LOSe A OCEAN JOY ,
4 A TEAR OF PAIN!!!!!!!...
IT NOW FAIR......
DRY THE TEAR N ENJOY THE OCEAN...

1 MUST SEPARATE,
FROM THIER UNDERSTANDIN
2 UNDERSTAND..

✦ ✦ ✦

UNDERSTANDIN GIVE U
BLESSIN IF U PICK WISELY...

✦ ✦ ✦

WISELY IS 2 UNDERSTAND...........

✦ ✦ ✦

finance is the richness of the heart..........

✦ ✦ ✦

people always told me i was nothing,

Angel Ramos

2day i found something completely special.
in i made everything out of it.....................self.....

♦ ♦ ♦

self mean alot if u don't look at other thing
...................being responsible ......

♦ ♦ ♦

bless is the 1st step 2 the ending
plane, train, bus, car, run, track, walk, dose not matter.
the matter is conquering the beginnin..
so u can b safe in the end........

♦ ♦ ♦

BLESS B THE WALK THAT
WE DECIDE ON OUR DECISIONS........

♦ ♦ ♦

FAITH IS MADE IN OUR THOUGHT,
BUT CREATED ON OUR DESCISIONS....................

♦ ♦ ♦

ESSENCE IS MADE AS
WE WALK OUR THINKING.......................

✦ ✦ ✦

GLUE IS MADE OUT OF
2 INGREDIENT,
N ONE DESCISION,,,,,,,,,,,,,,,,,,
CRAZY UUUUUUU.

✦ ✦ ✦

iN A BTFUL SKY, THERE R RAINBOW N A POT OF GOLD AT THE END.
JUS LIKE THE HEART IT'S FULL WITH BTFUL WORDS,,,,,,,

THE 1ST STEP IS THE SAME
AS THE LAST STEP,
DON'T LET YR MONDAY
CONQUER YR FRIDAY
THEY BOTH THE SAME ,,,,,,
CALLED TIME N JOY

✦ ✦ ✦

IF U WANT THE RULER,
U MUST LEARN WAT IS AN INCH ..
The measurement of understanding

✦ ✦ ✦

A WISH IS LIKE MATERIAL,
U CAN MAKE IT REAL...............SELF

Angel Ramos

✦ ✦ ✦

IF U DEFINE THE TRUTH ,
U FOUND THE TRIAL OF THE PATH
...........................SELF.....

✦ ✦ ✦

IF U PEBBLES 2GETHER U CREATED A MOUTAIN.
IF U PUT WORDS 2GETHER U CREATED YR SELF....................
SELF......
USE WORDS AS FLASHLIGHT,
SO YR HEART CAN GIVE U THE PATH.......

✦ ✦ ✦

HOW CAN WE THROW A STONE FAR,
IF WE DON'T KNO WAT A STONE IS.
A STONE IS A WORD,
THAT IS HIDDEN UNDERNEATH THE HEART.
IF WE PICK UP THE HEART N LOOK AROUND U FIND,
N THEN U MAY THROW THE STONE.
A STONE IS A WORD ONE CREATES

✦ ✦ ✦

BRINNG WAT U CAN --NOTHING--,
N I WILL GIVE WAT U NEED --EVERYTHING—
..................SELF........

✦ ✦ ✦

if u open yr heart
it's rite there.....

✦ ✦ ✦

INTERVIEW IS WAT U SEE IN WORDS
THE PRESENTS OF YR HEART...

SPOT WHERE YR HEART IS,,
NOT WHERE YR MIND GOES!!!!!!

✦ ✦ ✦

LOVE WILL EAZZZZZZZZZZZZ ANY PAIN...
IF ONE READ THE SENTENCE IN WORDS
WRITTEN BY DECISION OF SECONDS..........

✦ ✦ ✦

WATCH OUT 4 FALLIN EMOTIONS
.....................OUCHHHHHHHHH....

✦ ✦ ✦

BEHAVIOR CREATES SMILE ,
IF WE KNO WAT BEHAVIOR COME FROM
!!!!!!!!!!!!!!!!!!!!!!! SILIENCE CREATE BEHAVIOR

✦ ✦ ✦

CONDITIONS GIVES UNDERSTANDING,
IF U KNO YR CONDITION...

✦ ✦ ✦

BLESS WALK THE PATH
IF U GIVE IT LIGHT

OUR NAME IS SPELL
WITH A >>H-E-A-R-T<<

✦ ✦ ✦

A STEP IS A BLESSIN
BY DEFINNNING THE HEART

✦ ✦ ✦

ECHO GIVE U SOUND,
THE HEART GIVE IT LOVE...

✦ ✦ ✦

FREEDOM IS A WORD'S OF BEAUTY
.... SO FEEL IT....

✦ ✦ ✦

people WHO PUT WOOD IN WORDS
MADE GET BURN ,INSTEAD OF ENLIGHTMENT....

✦ ✦ ✦

EZZZZZZZZZZZZZ THY MIND,
SO THE BODY RELAXXXX COMFY..

✦ ✦ ✦

EZZZZZZZZZZZZZ THY MIND, SO THE BODY RELAXXXX
COMFY..

WALK SOOO U MAY B THERE
..........LOVE R THE STEP .....

✦ ✦ ✦

as long as SECOND sound ,
i will live that walk.....

✦ ✦ ✦

MILK NURTURE BABYS,
AS MUSIC NURTURE ADULTS...
I TAKE MY WITH PRESENT..

✦ ✦ ✦

ENLIGHTMENT IS THE NOTES

Angel Ramos

OF JOY THAT THE HEART MAKES......

✦ ✦ ✦

WALK WAT U FEEL,
SAY WAT U DON'T

✦ ✦ ✦

SECONDS PATH MADE B CALVE WITH LOVE
.... SO MAKE THE ROAD 2- DAY..........

SEEING MAKES PATH,
SEE YRSELF SO U
DON'T TRIP ON YR EMOTIONS.......

✦ ✦ ✦

PEACE IS LIKE,
HOW U MAKE THE BED.
ONLY THE HEART
DEFINE THE TRUTH

✦ ✦ ✦

WILL IS THE STRENGHT
2 WALK THE PATH.....

✦ ✦ ✦

WALL R EASY 2 WALK THROUGH
JUS BELIEVE IN SELF.....
DON'T LET WORDS BE WALLS

✦ ✦ ✦

WHY FIGHT NOTHING
THAT NOT THERE....EMOTIONS

✦ ✦ ✦

B-CAREFUL WAT U PICK UP,
IT'S MEND 2 CREATE EMOTIONS....

EZ SECOND'S MADE OF COMFORT...
DEFINE BY THE HEART......

✦ ✦ ✦

BLA, BLA, BLA, BLA, -
ARE EMOTIONS.
MMMM, MMMM, MMMM, -
ARE UNDERSTANDING
..........DARKNESS - N – LIGHTNESS .....

✦ ✦ ✦

ALL FLAVOR R
MADE WITH INGRIDIENT,
ALL MEDITATION N PRAYER R

MADE BY THINKIN...................
BELIEVE N B AWAKEN..

✦ ✦ ✦

ONLY A BEGINNING MAKES THE END.
END OF THAT BEGINNING.........
The starting ENDING................

✦ ✦ ✦

UNDERSTANDING IS ACCEPTANCE,
NOT DECEPTIONS
........CONCEPT OF BEING...................
 >>> ((THERE))<<<
BUT WE CHOOSE 2 SEEK
EVERYWHERE ELSE.
THE THING IS HOW CAN
WE LOSE SOMETHING
THAT'S IMPOSSIBLE 2 LOSE.
EMOTIONS BLOCK OUT
THE TRUE VALUE OF OUR SELF.................
EVERYTHING IS FOUND
IN SELF VALUE THAT.......

✦ ✦ ✦

A DAY IS JUS A DAY,
DONT ADD WORDS 2 IT
AND IT WOULD B A NICE SENTENCE
REGUARDLESS IT WILL PASS........

HAPPY ((SECONDS)) SUPRISE...

✦ ✦ ✦

UNDERSTANDING IS ACCEPTANCE,
NOT DECEPTIONS........
CONCEPT OF BEING........
UNDERSTANDING IS ACCEPTANCE,
NOT DECEPTIONS........
CONCEPT OF BEING........
SEE THE UNDERSTANDING,
N U HAVE YR RESULT...........
QUESTION N ANSWER OF SELF.....
WHAT WOULD I FIND IN A WORD......

✦ ✦ ✦

A SECOND CAN
DESTROY A DAY,
HE GAVE US 365 DAY
2 BLESS OURSELF.
WHEN WE LOOK
4 EMOTIONS
LIKE LOOKIN 4 A
NEEDLE IN A HAY STACK,
WHICH CAN MESS THE DAY.
B AWARE IT ONLY TAKE A
SEC 2 DESTROY A SIMPLE LIFE.........
TAKE CARE OF SECOND,
SECOND TAKE CARE OF LIFE..........

♦ ♦ ♦

CLIMB N U WILL SUCCEED,
SWIN N U WILL REACH............
THF FINDIN OF SELF
SIMPLE<<<----------→   > = <<----------------- >>SELF

♦ ♦ ♦

WHEN THE HEARTS ECHOOOO!!!!
THE EYES SHOULD RESPOND...........
AWARENESS...

♦ ♦ ♦

WHEN THE LOVE IS CARRIED,
THE FAITH FOLLOW LIKE
A SHADOW 2 PROTECT IT FALL...................
ESSENCE N FAITH..

♦ ♦ ♦

I SWIM 2 LIVE,
 NOT SWIM 2 DROWN.............
B-WARE OF EMOTIONS
THEY WEIGHT LIKE MOUNTAINS.

♦ ♦ ♦

walkin with bless is the

demanding of understanding,
n the mandatory of the heart.
only emtions can b rudenness of it,
n throw the focus 2 blindness.

VISION IS THE SOUND EYES HEAR,
WHEN THE HEART TUNES
ITSELF WITH MODESTY....................
PURE HARMONY.....

✦ ✦ ✦

MANDATORY IS EVERYTHING 2 CLAIM 2,
IF YR HEART AINT EVERYTHING.
TELL SELF WAT IS REALLY EVERYTHNG!!!....
THE START OF A FINISH LINE, AS MIRROR....................

✦ ✦ ✦

TIME IS NOT CLOCK,
OR WATCH.
TIME IS ONESELF
COMPOSE OF MUSIC...............
WAT A SWEET SOUND 1 IS.......

✦ ✦ ✦

CARING IS WATCHING OUT 4,
BEING THERE 4,
PROTECTING 2 MAKE
SURE EVERYTHINGITS O.K.

BEING SECURE OF
SURROUNDING ETC, ETC,
.....TAKE CARE OF THY HEART .....

✦ ✦ ✦

PRAISE B YR WALK
AS U STEP INTO
BLISS OF NOTHING....
SOMETHING IS THE SHORE
OF HORIZON EVERYTHING
ESSENCE THE CREATER
UNDERSTANDING AS BUILDER
WORDS BELIEVING AS MIRROR

✦ ✦ ✦

EVOLUTIONS :: is it the myth of theology..
is it the theory of mythology,
or is it the TRUTH OF UNDERSTANDING......................WORDS,,,,,

✦ ✦ ✦

LOVE CAN HIDE UNDER UNDERSTANDING
N COLOR IT SO B AWARE.................

✦ ✦ ✦

PAIN desire COMFORT.....

♦ ♦ ♦

WOW!!!! WORDS SURVIVE
THE WRATH OF THE EMOTIONS...
THERE IS AN ESSENCE......HAHAHAHAHA
THE AWAKENNING COME
IN DIFFERENT COLORS,
UNDERSTANDING IS
THE CLEAR N SIMPLE.......

♦ ♦ ♦

ESSENCE TUDOR UNDERTSTANDING
THINK!!!! THERE 4 I AM,
SO THERE 4 R U ......

♦ ♦ ♦

THE AWAKENNING COME
IN DIFFERENT COLORS,
UNDERSTANDING IS
THE CLEAR N SIMPLE .....

♦ ♦ ♦

PRODUCT LIKE ESSENCE,
DIVINE, GLORY, R FORM N MADE.....
TRY THEM THEY R FREE.....
I AM ALSO A CLIENT FREE ADMIN..

✦ ✦ ✦

I AM THAT PARTICLE,
THATS IN THE AIR.
STRONG LIKE A FEATHER,
N WEAK AS A MOUNTAIN. .... I--AM--U.....

I AM THAT PARTICLE,
THATS IN THE AIR.
STRONG LIKE A FEATHER,
N WEAK AS A MOUNTAIN.
.... I--AM--U.....

✦ ✦ ✦

STEP B 4 WALKIN,
UNDERSTANDING B 4 DECIDING!!!!!

✦ ✦ ✦

DISTANCE IS THE PATH 2 DEFINE
THE NEAREST DIFFERENT THE
(U) N THE (I)
.... 2 STORY 1 ANSWER

✦ ✦ ✦

MAKE A MATH SOLUTION IN-2
A SENTENCE MIRROR......

✦ ✦ ✦

PATH COME IN ALOTS OF COLORS,
UNDERSTANDING COMES IN 1 FLAVOR
.......>- understanding of think -<……...
SCHOOL BUSES COME WITH ALOTS OF CHILDREN,
A BODY COMES WITH ALOTS OF EMOTIONS............

✦ ✦ ✦

BEAUTY COMES WITH ALOTS OF EMOTION,
EXCEPT THE 1 U FIND IN SELF.....

✦ ✦ ✦

i am yr pain,
i am yr joy...................
i am the freedom.

✦ ✦ ✦

LIFE IS SOOOOOOOOOOOOO!! BTFUL
SOOOOOOOOOOOOO WALK IT...................
IN THE HEART......

✦ ✦ ✦

A QUIET PERSON IS LIKE A MIRROR,
EVERYBODY ALWAYS POINTING AT THEMMMMMM

♦ ♦ ♦

A NICE WALK IS ONLY A TEAR AWAY....

♦ ♦ ♦

IF U CAN PATCH A BROKEN HEART,
WITH A TEAR. U JUS DEFINE THE WORD JOY.........
EACH THREAD OF THE FABRIC IS THE BEINg
...................THREAD R WORDS...........

♦ ♦ ♦

WALK AS YOU SEE,
SEE THE WALK
YOU SEE IN SELF....

♦ ♦ ♦

LEGOS COME IN PIECES,
HEARTS COMES IN WORDS...

♦ ♦ ♦

SEE WHAT IS THERE,
LOVE WHAT IS THERE.
B WHAT IS THERE SELF......

♦ ♦ ♦

2 CLIMB WE HAVE 2 REACH,
2 SWIM WE HAVE 2 STRETCH.
2 UNDERSTAND 1 MUST LOVE...

✦ ✦ ✦

THE SPIRIT IS IN THE WORDS,
THE ESSENCE IS IN SOUND.
THE UNDERSTANDIN IS IN THE BELIEVER.

watch where u walk,
and yr heart will b clear.
as the light of the PATH..

✦ ✦ ✦

poisons r words
that don't fit the HEART.....

✦ ✦ ✦

FUNNY THING THE WRATH OR
WIND OF LIFE IS TRYIN 2 GET,
AND WAT I SAY 2 THAT.
WHAT ELSE U GOT 4 ME IN STORE.
REMEMBER I HAVE WORDS
THAT PROTECT LIKE
LOVE, RESPECT, VALUE, ETC ET.
 I REFUSE 2 LET U TOUCH ME
ANY MORE HOLD THAT 4 SIZE........
BLESS B WORDS THAT GIVE STRENGHT....

Angel Ramos

❖ ❖ ❖

IF U CARRY MY WORDS I GUARANTEE YOU,
LOVE MY SELF, RESPECT MY SELF, VALUE MY SELF.
YOU WILL CARRY YR HEART................................
2 BELIEVE THATIS BLESS,
JUS BELIEVE THAT IS BLESS
...................SELF...

❖ ❖ ❖

ANOTHER WIND OF THE WRATH AT ME,,,,,,
AINT HAPPENNIN,,,,,,,LOVE RESPECT, VALUE.....................
YR ARM R 2 SHORT 2 BOX WITH essence...

❖ ❖ ❖

CREATIONS R ILLUsION
WHEN IT COMES 2 EMOTIONS.....

❖ ❖ ❖

WALK THE DISTANCE YR HEART
NEEDS YOU 2 DECIDE.........

❖ ❖ ❖

HEARTS BRINGS JOY,
BUT YOU MUST REACH...........
SELF FINDIN....

THE DISCOVERY CHANNEL : : >
LOOKIN 4 WORDS THAT DEFINE YR TRUE HEAT
---------------------SELF--------------

✦ ✦ ✦

I RATHER CRY A TEAR
THAT HAS UNDERSTANDIN,
THAN 2 CRY A RIVER
WITH NO MEANNING..

✦ ✦ ✦

IF U TOUCH,
MAKE SURE THEY R
NOT ATTACHABLE,,,,,,,,WORDS

✦ ✦ ✦

the sounds of words may
feel like wave or wind,
dangerous 2
the fragile heart...

✦ ✦ ✦

wow.........
.........substitube.....4 ....
...... simple......
HAPPINESS IS SEEING IT......

♦ ♦ ♦

RADDLES R 4 BABY ,
NOT 4 ADULT
STOP SHAKIN YR HEAD...

♦ ♦ ♦

PRODUCT R DONE BY CARE....

♦ ♦ ♦

LOVE COME IN HEART SHAPE,
SOME R SWEET N SOME R (------)
NAW I'M NOT GOING 2 SAY IT...

♦ ♦ ♦

:)) i am FINE . < > . really fine....

♦ ♦ ♦

B WHILE U WALK,
PRESENT WAT U R.

♦ ♦ ♦

GIVE A SMILE 2 THE ONE IN NEED OUR HEART.
SO THE LIGHT OF THE PATH BRIGHTED FOR OTHER
---------------SELF-------------- MOVing

✦ ✦ ✦

goin 2 play in the darkness
a little bit b nice 2 self

✦ ✦ ✦

SPECIALS EFFECT ARE EMOTIONSS...........

✦ ✦ ✦

COME TO MY WORDS
SO I CAN PROTECT YOU
ON THE SILENT JOURNEY
THAT FULL WITH NOISE..........

✦ ✦ ✦

WHY PUT WEIGHT
ON THE WORD'S,
WHEN YOU KNOW
YOU CAN'T CARRY THEM.

✦ ✦ ✦

PUDDLES SURPOSE 2 BE FUN, NOT SAD....
CARRY YOUR WORDS,
DON'T LET THEM CARRY YOU....

✦ ✦ ✦

IF THE ROAD IS THAT WAY,
WHY DO YOU TELL YOURSELF
2 GO THAT WAY.
WHEN YOU KNOW
THE ROAD IS THAT WAY...........

✦ ✦ ✦

if we feed the rite meannin 2 words.
the light of the words get brighter

✦ ✦ ✦

CARRY WORDS OF BLESSIN, N FAITH.
THEY COME IN HANDY IN THE
PRESENTS OF NEEDS NOT WANT......

✦ ✦ ✦

WORDS OF NEEDS GIVES YOU LIGHT,

✦ ✦ ✦

................TALES OF 2 CITIES................
ALL WORDS ARE EMPTY CAN YOU 4-FILL THEM,
START WITH THE WORD > SELF <.............

✦ ✦ ✦

IN THE BLISS OF THE UNIVERSE THERE ARE PARTICLE,

AND THOSE PARTICLE CAN ONLY BE FOUND ON EARTH
…..............................SELF..

♦ ♦ ♦

PEACE 2 THE WORLD AND YR HEART.....

♦ ♦ ♦

LOVE, RESPECT, VALUE,
THE FOUNDATION OF THE HEART......

♦ ♦ ♦

SEE YR ESSENSE IS HARDER ,
THAN TOUCHIN THE SKY...................
THINK, NOW THERE GOES YR ESSENSE
IN THE PRESENT OF THINKIN..

♦ ♦ ♦

EVERY SECOND THERE IS,
IS ONLY ONE PRESENT.....
IF U CAN THINK WITH
YOUR EYE CLOSE,
IMAGINE WAT YOU
CAN DO WHEN
2 ARE OPEN N
YOU AWARE OF THAT
.........LOVE.........

✦ ✦ ✦

EVERY SECOND THERE IS,
IS ONLY ONE PRESENT....

✦ ✦ ✦

THE FINE LINE BETWEEN
MADNESS AND SANITY IS SELF........

✦ ✦ ✦

UNDERSTANDING BRINGS HARVEST,
 EMOTIONS BRINGS STARVATION

✦ ✦ ✦

THE WALK OF LIFE
IS 2 EXPERIENCE
THE PRESENTS OF BEING
IN THE MOMENTS OF PRESENTS................
WHAT IS THE DIFFERENTS BETWEEN TIME, AND TIME
......................................NOTHING JUS PRESENTS..

✦ ✦ ✦

LAYERS CAN HIDE THE TRUTH,,,,,,,,,,,,,,,,,,,,,
Pilling a sponge..................
EMOTIONS CUP..........................

✦ ✦ ✦

DON'T BELIEVE, JUS BELIEVE
...........SIMPLE.........

✦ ✦ ✦

THERE IS NOTHING IN THE DARK,
THERE IS NOTHING IN THE LIGHT.
NOW THERE EVERYTHING IN UNDERSTANDING..

✦ ✦ ✦

PUT A MIRROR IN FRONT OF YOU,
AND TELL ME WHAT YOU SEE.
DON'T START WITH YOUR SELF,
START WITH YOUR TEAR......................SELF...........

✦ ✦ ✦

WHY IS IT THAT WE SEE THE WAR IN THE DARK,
BUT NOT IN THE LIGHT................................SELF.....
DARKNESS IS THINNER THAN A PENCIL DOT,
DON'T MARINATE IT. IT MAY TURN INTO DARKNESS............

✦ ✦ ✦

THERE ARE 2 HEART BURN IN LIFE,
ONE CAUSE BY ACID THE OTHER BY EMOTIONS............

LIFE IS LIKE A ROSE BTFUL,
IF U HOLD IT RITE.
NOW DON'T LET THE
EMOTIONS THORN YOU........

✦ ✦ ✦

WORDS ARE BOUQUETS
OF FLOWERS IN LIFE……..

✦ ✦ ✦

IF I GIVE YOU A VASE 2 MAKE A BOUQUET,
WHICH WORDS WOULD YOU CHOOSE
…………………………..VASE IS SELF,,,,,,,,

✦ ✦ ✦

SAFETY RULED WATCH OUT
4 CANDY THEY MOVE..
OPINIONS IS LIKE MONEY ,
PURE EXAMPLE::>
 A MAN SAID WHOSE FACE
YOU SEE IN THE COIN.
GIVE 2 CEASAR
WHAT BELONG 2 CEASER,
GIVE ME WHAT BELONG 2 ME
………..UNDERSTANDING…….

Love is strange it comes in
all flavor sour n sweet.
desicion, descision..............

❖ ❖ ❖

UNDERSTANDING GIVE CREATIVITY
OF THE TRUTH ONE NEEDS 2 SEEK
..................SELF...............

❖ ❖ ❖

TEAR CLEAR THE THE LIGHT,
 WHY COVER THE LIGHT WITH
PAIN THAT CREATE DARKNESS...................
SIMPLE:::: A SIMPLE WORD
GIVE ALL U NEEDS IN LIFE 2 UNDERSTAND
THE PATH THAT WAS MADE 4 YOU 2 FIND
 AND SEEK SO THAT WAY YOU CAN RELAX AT YOUR
COMFORT OF YOUR PRESENT......................
SIMPLE WORDS THAT ALL HONEST JUS BELIVE
.........................WORDS OF THE LORDS.....

❖ ❖ ❖

WHY DO YOU CRY,
WHEN YOU LOV YOURSELF...

❖ ❖ ❖

TIME IS VALUE DON'T
SPEND IT ON EVRYTHING,
SPEND IT ON NOTHING

✦ ✦ ✦

REASON 4 CAUSES NOTHING,
CAUSES 4 REASON EVRYTHING

✦ ✦ ✦

VERSUS-VS-VERSUS,
I AM, I AM.............I AM……….am
CLIMB THE DISTANCE YOU
DON'T SEE IN FRONT OF YOU..................SELF

✦ ✦ ✦

IF YOU CAN LEAP OVER THE
SMALLEST WALL IN THE WORLD,
\YOU JUS REACH THE LIGHT...

✦ ✦ ✦

DON'T ASK 4 IT
IF YOU CAN'T GET OUT
.........DARKNESS..........

✦ ✦ ✦

THINK THAT'S ALL I ASK OF YOU............A.K.A......SELF

✦ ✦ ✦

IN THE OCEAN OF SOMETHING,
THERE A PATH OF NOTHING.
 THAT GIVE YOU EVERYTHING IN PRESENT................SELF

✦ ✦ ✦

SMILE N FEEL THAT THE
LIGHT WE LOOKING FOR....
WALK THE LONGEST DISTANCE,
THAT DISTANCE IS YOUR PATH.
THAT DISTANCE IS YOUR LIGHT.
THAT DISTANCE START NOW,
WHICH IS EVERY SECOND YOU CAN HOLD ON 2
................................DISTANCE ARE SECOND IN SELF

✦ ✦ ✦

SMILE N FEEL THAT THE LIGHT WE LOOKING FOR...

✦ ✦ ✦

GRAB YOUR WORDS
 THEY WILL MAKE A BIG
 DIFFERENT IN YOUR LIFE.
WARNNING:: DON'T LET THE WORDS GRAB YOU
...........AWARENESS......

Angel Ramos

✦ ✦ ✦

HOW CAN YOU GIVE YRSELF LOVE,
WHEN YOU LOOKIN AT EVETYHING.
WARNNING EVERYTHING IS LOVE,
SO GIVE IT 2 YR SELF

✦ ✦ ✦

REMEMBER EVERYTHING AND NOTHING,
ARE POWER IN THE MOMENTS OF SELF....

B WALK..................................SIMPLE

✦ ✦ ✦

ever heard the story of a FISH
that use2 swim in the sea of essence.
it decided 2 venture in2 the land a.k.a body.
in the land the fish cannot servive
it try the best it can,
but there the essence in l
and wasn't the same essense it needs
2 live as it was in the sea.
the essense in the sea gave it joy, happinness,will.
the essence in the land was now the same.
the fish felt empty, lonely, it felt like darkness was upon itself.
it seem pain was all over. 2 shorten the story the FISH return HOME 2 SELF
......................THY--SELF...................

✦ ✦ ✦

USE WORDS AS WALKIN,
JUS AS WORDS ARE USED AS SPELLIN.........CORRECT.

✦ ✦ ✦

2 DEFINE THE MEANNIN OF LOVE ,
 YOU MUST TRUELY QUESTIONS YOUR SMILE
 ....LOVE MY SELF...

what is was, was was was............
CAN YOU READ THE WORD SELF
................IT'S A REAL GOOD BOOK......

✦ ✦ ✦

IF YOU CAN TRAIN YRSELF 2 SILENCE WORDS,
YOU CAN TRAIN YRSELF 2 MASTER THEM......................
UNDERSTANDING THE WORDS OF SELF......

✦ ✦ ✦

CLIMBING IS LIKE FALLIN,
UNTIL YOU KNOW WAT YOU CLIMBING
..........................SELF IS THE LADDLER OF LIFE

✦ ✦ ✦

MAY PEACE BE YOUR REST,

SO YOU CAN WAKE UP WITH
THE LIGHT IN YOUR SMILE.......

✦ ✦ ✦

mercy, compassion, 4-giveness
form of bonding with self
how thinkin can give you love within yrself
...................THINK .....

✦ ✦ ✦

understanding WILL LIGHT YOUR DARKNESS
...................SEE THINKIN

✦ ✦ ✦

peaceful mind is always
in a great spiritual person.....be one

✦ ✦ ✦

WALK WITH PEACE SO
YOUR STEP MAY BE LIGHTER....................COMFORT

✦ ✦ ✦

NOGETIATION IS EVERYTHING YOU,
 DONT WANT 2 DO WITH SELF

✦ ✦ ✦

WHAT IS THE MEANNIN ------------ SIMPLE --------- TELL ME,
WHAT IS THE MEANNIN.................AAAAAHHHHH, I'VE GOT
IT. THANK YOU...............SELF

✦ ✦ ✦

WHY IS NO NEEDS 2 BE ASK..............
2 DEFINE YOU NEED A MEANNIN.
 COULD THAT MEANNIN BE, YOU,
ME, US, THEM, WE, ALL OR SELF
.........UNDERSTANDIN ALL IN ON

✦ ✦ ✦

THANK LIFE 4 THE MOMENTS OF THE PRESENTS
YOU HAVE GIVEN ME 2 ENJOY AT YOUR BEIN

✦ ✦ ✦

2 DEFINE YOU NEED A reason.
COULD THAT reason. BE, YOU, ME, US, THEM, WE, ALL OR
SELF........................UNDERSTANDIN ALL IN ONE

✦ ✦ ✦

IMAGINE AN EMPTY FISH TANK.
YOU FILL IT WITH ROCKS SOME SAND,
AND MORE STUFF.

ADD WATER AND SOME FISHES,
NOW YOU GOT LIFE.
WHAT WOULD ADD 2 AN EMPTYBODY
2 MAKE IT'S PRESENT BE TRU

✦ ✦ ✦

WHY IS NO NEEDS 2 BE ASK............

✦ ✦ ✦

WALK THE DISTANCE YOU SEE.
THAT DISTANCE IS THE JOUNEY IN SELF.
BECOME THE DISTANCE YOU CAN REACH

✦ ✦ ✦

SEEING YRSELF AS YOU WALK
THE JOUNEY THAT WAS MENT 2 BE.
IS THE BURST OF BLESSEN THAT BEEN
MADE 4 YOU IN THE PRESENTS
OF MOMENT THAT ARE YOUR

✦ ✦ ✦

UNDERSTANDIN GIVES THE PICTURE OF LIFE,
NOT THE COLORS YOU PICK

✦ ✦ ✦

Renaissance of Butterflies

KNOWLEDGE GIVE A COMPLEX WORLD,
UNDERSTANDING GIVES A SIMPLE UNIVERSE

✦ ✦ ✦

ADD LIFE 2 YR SMILE CAUSE THATS
WHERE YOUR UNDERSTANDIN COME FROM,
AND THAT YOU

✦ ✦ ✦

MAY ALL THE WORDS DEFINE THE ONE ======== YOU
HOLD HANDS WITH YOUR HEART,
SO THEY CAN SEE HOW STRONG HIS WORDS ARE

✦ ✦ ✦

IN THE BLISS OF THE OCEAN
THE SEEN CAN STILL BE SEEN.................SELF

✦ ✦ ✦

THE SEARCH IS THE ENDING
WHEN YOU FIND THE BLESSIN THAT'S YOU

✦ ✦ ✦

IF YOU THINK YOU GETTIN OVER ON ME,
WATCH OUT. IF YOU KEEP BULLING ME,
WATCH OUT. IF YOU THINK YOU'RE SMART,

Angel Ramos

WATCH OUT. YOU ONLY ROBBING YOURSELF
FROM THE PRESENTS OF YOUR TRUE SPIRIT

✦ ✦ ✦

THERE ARE 2 BALANCING ACT IN LIFE CALLED ESSENCE.
ONE ACT IS DARK, AND THE OTHER IS LIGHT.
WHICH PART OF THE ACT YOU RATHER BE.

✦ ✦ ✦

part of livin is 1 2 b
............simple............
feel it b-4 yr mind goes........
REACH WHERE U THINK THERE NO TOUCH.
HEAR WHERE YOU THINK THERE IS NO VOICES.
SEE THE SITE YOU CAN SEE .... SELF

✦ ✦ ✦

YOUR WORDS IS WHAT YOU WALK
EVERY SECOND IN THE PRESENTS REALITY OF SELF

✦ ✦ ✦

IF I WALK TO SEE, WHY CAN I SEE TO WALK...........

✦ ✦ ✦

IF I WALK WHY DON'T YOU FOLLOW,

IF I STAY WHY DO YOU MOVE
...............CAUSES OF THINKIN

✦ ✦ ✦

THINKING WITHOUT UNDERSTANDING,
IS STEP WITHOUT WALKING
...............LOST HERIZON

✦ ✦ ✦

BEAUTY WITHOUT COMFORT, IS A PATH WITHOUT LIGHT
...............INNER CLAIM

THE SOURCE OF A BLESSIN,
IS THE TRUE UNDERSTANDING OF THE SMILE

✦ ✦ ✦

A SMILE IS LIKE FEELIN HEAVEN N WHY,
CAUSE OF A SMILE ARE MADE BY UNDERSTANDING
HOW YOU SEE THE WORDS IN YOU
AND YOU MADE IT INTO A REALITY BY JUS THINKING
...............LOVE, RESPECT, VALUE, BELIEVE, HAPPINESS,
JOY, GLORY, BLESS, FAITH, TRUTH, 4-FILLMENT, PLEASURE,
ACHIEVEMEMT, CONQUER, REACH, CLAIM, MADE, ACCOM-
PLISH,
ACCEPTANCE,RULED,ETC,ETC,...............IN SELF...............
THE LIGHT THAT YOU MADE IN A SECOND BY THINK

❖ ❖ ❖

YOU ARE THE STRENGTH OF YOUR WORDS,
BELIEVE THAT YOU ARE THE HOLDER OF THEM
AND YOU ARE THE DECK OR YOUR HANDS, SO DEAL YOUR
WALK...................SELF

❖ ❖ ❖

BELIEVING IS TO PLUG IN TO UNDERSTANDING,,,,,,,,,,,,,,,,,,

❖ ❖ ❖

HOW 2 SEAL A SMILE, BY UNDERSTANDING

❖ ❖ ❖

the reflection, give a hug in return is the blessin n faith.

I SAY YOU ARE A GLASS HOUSE THAT THINKS ,
THAT IS A WALL

❖ ❖ ❖

LET IT BE WHO U TRUELY ARE..........................SIMPLE NOT COMPLEX

❖ ❖ ❖

SIMPLE DEFINE WHO YOU ARE,

NOT COMPLEX THAT YOU WANNA BE........

✦ ✦ ✦

ANGEL AND DEMANS MANIPILATIONS OF WORD

................OOOOOOPPPSS DID I SAY THAT .....

✦ ✦ ✦

COMFORT 2 THE HEART,

IS SEEING BEIN IN THE MOMENT OF SELF

✦ ✦ ✦

CONQUERING IS SEE WHAT YOU CAN EXPRESS

✦ ✦ ✦

IT'S BEAUTIFUL 2 CRY TEARS 4 THE BETTER BEIN

...............WORDS ARE STRENGTH AS FOLLOW

STRENGHT IS THE REACH YOU SEE B-4 WE ACT
..........................PRESENTS OF WORDS

✦ ✦ ✦

WORDS COULD BLIND THE VISION OF ITS TURE COLORS,
COLORS R THE WORDS NOT THE SAYING
...............PEACE BE ALL'S WORDS.....

✦ ✦ ✦

WORDS ARE THE BLINDFoLD,
LOOKIN IS THE VISIONS…..

✦ ✦ ✦

THE DAY IS HERE, THE DAY IS THE FOCUS OF THE SEC.
CAUSE SECONDS WILL MAKE YR DAYS............................
POWER OF MOMENTS........

✦ ✦ ✦

THE DAY IS HERE, THE DAY IS THE FOCUS OF THE SEC.
CAUSE SECONDS WILL MAKE YR DAYS............................
POWER OF MOMENTS........

✦ ✦ ✦

GIVE WHAT LIFE ABOUT, AND IT'S START BY LOVING OUR-

SELF.
YOU WON'TBELIEVE THE RESPONSE WE WILL GET FROM SELF...................LIGHT...
THE POWER 2 GIVE IS 2 BE,,,,,,,,

✦ ✦ ✦

THE TRUE LIGHT IS 2 LOOK AT SELF...........

✦ ✦ ✦

B-E-L-I-E-V-E SEVEN LETTER,
WEEK SEVEN DAYS.
WALK WITH A LETTER EACH DAY
....................AND UNDERSTANDING

✦ ✦ ✦

AMAZING GRACE, NOW THAT'S A FEELING TO EXPERIENCE
......................SELF

✦ ✦ ✦

GIVE YOU THE YOU, YOU NEED!!!.....................SELF

✦ ✦ ✦

NOMATTER HOW MUCH IT RAINS,
SMILES WILL ALWAYS SHINE.......................PEACE

✦ ✦ ✦

TO GO IS, IS TO KNOWLEDGE,
WHAT COMES IS TO UNDERSTANDIN
……………..SELF

4-FILLING THE CATCHING OF THE TRUTH OF UNDERSTANDING………………SELF

✦ ✦ ✦

UNDERSTANDING OPENS,
KNOWLEDGES CLOSES
……………SELF

✦ ✦ ✦

UNDERSTANDING PICKS, KNOWLEDGE SEARCHES……………
SELF

✦ ✦ ✦

UNDERSTANDING STANDS,
WHILES KNOWLEDGE WALKS
……………..SELF

✦ ✦ ✦

WE MADE LOOK AT WORDS WITH MEANNING, OR WE

MADE NOT.
NOW WHAT IS THE MEANNING..........................UNDERSTAND-
ING
THE RISK IN VIEW IS UNDERSTANDING
WHERE 2 FIND......................SELF

❖ ❖ ❖

THE LOOK IN SEEING,
IS THE VISIONS IN PRESENTS
.... SELF
LETS PICK UP ALL THE DARKNESS WE HAVE IN US,
LOOK UNDER IT AND WE WILL SEE THE LIGHT
.......................INNER SELF

❖ ❖ ❖

WHY WE B____!! WHEN WE PUT OUR FOOT IN YOUR MOUTH,
KNOWING IF FIT PERFECT......................SELF AWARE

❖ ❖ ❖

WHY WE B____!! WHEN WE PUT OUR FOOT IN YOUR MOUTH,
KNOWING IF FIT PERFECT......................SELF AWARE

❖ ❖ ❖

IF YOU CAN TOUCH THE WORDS IN THE DARKNESS,

MAY YOU MADE UNDERSTAND THEM IN THE LIGHT
......................SELF DISCOVER
RELATIONS FIND SELF , AND COMMUNICATE......................
TRUE UNDERSTANDING IN BONDIN

♦ ♦ ♦

THE MOMENTS IN NOTHING,
HELP YOU SEE EVERYTHING IN SELF.
IF YOU TOUCH YOUR UNDERSTANDING
WITH YOUR PRESENT CALLED ....SIMPLE

♦ ♦ ♦

PAIN + (-: = SELF...................BALANCING AWARENESS

♦ ♦ ♦

THERE RITE THERE,
JESUS CHRIST RITE THERE
...........................SELF

♦ ♦ ♦

LOVE TO THE FINDING
.................................SELF

♦ ♦ ♦

SPELL LOVE, LISTEN TO THE SOUND OF IT

.........YOU JUST SPENT TIME IN SELF

✦ ✦ ✦

IF A REACH IS A DISTANCE,
WHAT IS THE FINDING IN THAT IN
THAT REACH.......................SELF

✦ ✦ ✦

DISTANCE IS THE PRESENT OF SELF,
IN THE NOW OF THE FUTURE

✦ ✦ ✦

TIME IS THE SAME IN THE BEFORE AND AFTER
..........CALLED NOW

✦ ✦ ✦

WHY CAN'T WE SEE THE PRESENT,
WHEN IT'S ALWAY THERE IN THE NOW
............................INNER SELF

✦ ✦ ✦

FEED THE SOUL WITH FOOD,
WITH THE 3 NUTRITIONS OF WORDS.
THAT FILL ITS PRESENTS.................
LOVE, RESPECT, VALUE

Angel Ramos

✦ ✦ ✦

a gift of a smile,
is like the light in the path
give them a smile,
and you gave them a shine.
give them a hug,
and you gave them a warmth.
give them a word,
and you gave them protections

✦ ✦ ✦

let me be your step,
SO YOU CAN BE MY WALK

✦ ✦ ✦

COME 2 ME, SO I CAN BE YOURS......................SELF

✦ ✦ ✦

PUT YOUR THOUGHT B-4 YOUR ACTIONS,
AND YR ACTIONS WILL BE YR THOUGHT...........SELF

✦ ✦ ✦

put a word in yr heart ,
like you do with yr wallet
and carry it..........................love

✦ ✦ ✦

THE COMPLEX OF LIFE,
THINKING OF IT.
THE SIMPLE IN LIFE,
UNDERSTANDING IT........................SELF

✦ ✦ ✦

JOY IS THE IS THE UNDERSTANDING OF SIMPLE.
ANGER IS THE UNDERSTANDING OF COMPLEX,,,,,,,,,,,,,,,,,,
THE 50/50,,,,,,,,,,,,,,,,,,,CHOICE

✦ ✦ ✦

I AM THE LIGHT OF YOUR PATH,
IF YOU LET ME BE YOUR TRAILS OF WORDS
................................WORDS 2 LIGHT

✦ ✦ ✦

MAY YOUR UNDERSTANDING,
DRY THE TEARS THAT ARE NOT CALL FOR
....................................BLESSIN

✦ ✦ ✦

MAY I COME TO YOU,
IN THE NEED OF SEARCH
.....................SELF

SEARCH 4 UNDERSTANDING IN THE PRESENTS OF THINKING,
BECOMES THE MOMENTS OF NOW......................SELF

♦ ♦ ♦

SEE ALL IN ONE.................SELF

♦ ♦ ♦

A SHADOW SCARE,
IS THE SHADOW THAT SAVES
......................ME AS IN SELF

♦ ♦ ♦

THOUGH I AM NOT THE MOMENTS YOU SEE,
I AM THE SECOND YOU PRESENT

♦ ♦ ♦

WORDS ARE ALWAYS UNDER THE PILE..................SELF

♦ ♦ ♦

YOU MAY HIDE IN DARKNESS WITH PAIN,
BUT THE REACH OF MY LIGHT IS ALWAYS THERE

♦ ♦ ♦

see all in nothing is seeing all

✦ ✦ ✦

come 2 me in love, so i can be yr glory...............self
THE POWER OF CREATIONS IS THE SAME
AS THE POWER OF BELIEVING, BELIEVE!!!

✦ ✦ ✦

BRING PEACE WITH YR UNDERSTANDING,
SO YR WORDS CAN RELAX IN THE PRESENT

✦ ✦ ✦

WHY SPILL A FULL CUP,
WHEN WE KNOW IS EMPTY

✦ ✦ ✦

MOUNTAIN MAY BE LGHTER,
THAN A FEATHER.
FEATHER MAY BE HEAVIER,
THAN A MOUTAIN.
GUESS WHAT WE ARE ALL
THE SAME IN ONE

✦ ✦ ✦

WORDS CAN WALK FAR,

Angel Ramos

WHEN YOU LIGHT ITS PATH

✦ ✦ ✦

please become my distance,
so i can be closeness

can i come closer,
if you walk away......................self

✦ ✦ ✦

THERES A SEARCH IN EVERYTHING,
THAT LEADS 2 ONE.......................UNDERSTANDIN

✦ ✦ ✦

MAY THE MASSES OF ONE,
BRIGHTEN THE PATH OF ALL

✦ ✦ ✦

WHY WE REST IN OUR PAIN,
WHEN THE TEARS IS OUR COMFORT

✦ ✦ ✦

IF YOU INCREASE YOUR UNDERSTANDING OF SELF,
YOUR ANGER IN SELF DECREASE

✦ ✦ ✦

GRAB EVERYTHING THATS
ALWAYS BEEN YOUR,
FAITH AND BLESS

✦ ✦ ✦

BLESS IS LOVE, FAITH IS RESPECT,
BELIEVE IS VALUE, AND YOU IS SELF
MAKING DECISIONS IN THE DARKNESS
WILL BE HARM 4 ONE SELF,
SO TURN THE LIGHT OF UNDERSTANDING
IN SELF BY THINKING.
SO THE PATH OF YOUR DECISIONS,
MAY BE CLEAR AND WHY

✦ ✦ ✦

THERE IS A SECRET IN ESSENCE AND SPIRIT,
THAT MAKE EVERYTHING CLEAR
............................SSSHHHHH!!!!..........SELF

✦ ✦ ✦

UNDERSTANDING CAN BE CLEAR OR DARK,
THAT UNDERSTANDING COMES FROM THINKING

✦ ✦ ✦

Angel Ramos

UNDERSTANDING CAN GIVE THE LOVE
WE BEEN LOOKING FOR,
OR THE LOVE THAT
ALWAYS BEEN THERE.............SELF

✦ ✦ ✦

a simple words can bring
down a complex empire,
not a simple one
simplify self,
and you have a kingdom

✦ ✦ ✦

LOVE IS A SIMPLE WORD IN SELF,
DON'T MAKE IT COMPLEX...............
TRUE KNOWING IS UNDERSTANDING

✦ ✦ ✦

YOU ARE THE WORDS THAT YOU CARRY,
YOU ARE THE LIGHT OF THE PATH................THINK

✦ ✦ ✦

THE SONGS 4 LOVE,
IS THE SOUND OF THE EARS BRING IN

✦ ✦ ✦

GRAB MY MISTAKES,
SO I CAN BE YOURS WORDS............SELF

✦ ✦ ✦

COME PLEASE BRING ME YOUR THINKING,
SO I CAN BE YOUR UNDERSTANDING...............SELF

✦ ✦ ✦

COME 2 THE UNDERSTANDING FROM NOTHING
COME 2 THE WALL THAT'S
NOT IN FRONT OF YOU,
ONLY INSIDE OF YOU...................SELF

✦ ✦ ✦

GIVE ME ALL AND I MEAN ALL
THE PAIN YOU HAVE IN A GRAIN,
SO I CAN GIVE YOU ALL
THE UNIVERSE IN A SIMPLE WORD......................SELF

✦ ✦ ✦

OPPOSITES ATTRACTS SELF
......................I AM, I AM. AM

✦ ✦ ✦

LOOK 4 WORDS

THE HAVE TRUE REASONGS,
AND FALSE MEANNING.
PUT THEM 2GETHER AND YOU WILL
FIND THE DARK SIDE OF WORDS,
AND THE LIGHT SIDE OF WORDS.
CHOOSE THE ONE THAT WILL
SHOW YOUR PATH OF SELF

✦ ✦ ✦

CLIMB THE LADDLE OF OF LIFE,
START WITH UNDERSTANDING
AND FOLLOW IT WITH SELF.
THE PUZZLE WILL BECOMES
B4 THE ACTIONS,
THAT IS THE ACTIONS
WITHIN IT SELF

✦ ✦ ✦

UNDERSTANDING IS THINKING,
NOT UNDERSTANDING UNDERSTAND
....................SELF

✦ ✦ ✦

OPEN A UNIVERSE THAT'S REAL.
OPEN A WORLD THAT'S REAL.
OPEN A PERSON THAT'S REAL,
Y-O-U................UNDERSTAND THY SELF

❖ ❖ ❖

HONESTLY---- GIVE YOUR
SELF A MINUTES,
AND SEE IF YOU
CAN FIND UNDERSTANDING.
AND IF YOU FOUND IT,
YOU JUS FOUND YOUR TRUTH SELF
...........NO BATTERIES INCLUDDED,
UNDERSTANDING RECHARGES IT SELF
A SMILE AND A HUG,
NOMATTER WHAT
FLAVOR IT COMES FROM.
IT'S CALLED A WALK IN
THE RITE P-A-T-H.........................
GIVIN IS THE RITE RECEIVING

❖ ❖ ❖

I - AM JOY, I - AM HURT,
THE UNDERSTANDING OF AM IN ALL.
THE COMPLETIONS OF SELF IN ALL IS (AM).
SO BE THE ALL THAT YOU ARE IN SELF

❖ ❖ ❖

lalalalalalalalalalalalalalallalalalalalalalalalalala.....reasons ti I

❖ ❖ ❖

Angel Ramos

WARM THE COLD WITH A HEART......

✦ ✦ ✦

COMMUNICATIONS IS WARMFUL.....

✦ ✦ ✦

is INSIDE
THERE ALWAYS
 AS NOW......
LOOK AT SELF
AND YOU DONT ABOUT THE TIME,
TIME IS YOURS..........................SELF

✦ ✦ ✦

STEP ON THE DISTANCE OR REACH,
SO WE CAN SEE THE NOW OF PRESENTS

✦ ✦ ✦

GRAB A WORD
AND REACH OVER IT,
WOULD COME IN HELPFUL

✦ ✦ ✦

LET ME BE THE PRESENT,
SO YOU KNOW THE DISTANCE IN NOW

......CALLED SECONDS

+ + +

THIS IS THE TIME
CALLED STRENGTH.
SO OUR NEW SECONDS
START WITH COMFORT,
AND SHINE LIGHT
IN OUR PATH,
THAT'S GIVING 2 US,
AS IT'S PROMISE
walk in self,
so you can be in self.

+ + +

give yr self the best breakfast,
by understanding yr words
........................fulfillment

+ + +

KEEP ON WITH THE BASIC IN LIFE JUS
........................LOVE

+ + +

IT'S NOT A FAR DISTANCE IN SELF

Angel Ramos

✦ ✦ ✦

WITH MY WIND UNDER YOUR WORDS,
THE LIGHT WILL BE BRIGHTER FOR YOUR PATH

✦ ✦ ✦

LET ME LIGHT THE CANDLE IN YOUR HEART,
SO YOU CAN FEEL ALL THE JOY THAT'S IN THERE

✦ ✦ ✦

GIVE YOUR SELF THE SMILE YOU DESERVE,
NOT THE ONE YOU THINK..........................UNDERSTAN-
DIN
BLESS, FAITH, WILL, IF YOU READ THIS THREE WORDS.
YOU JUS EARN THREE VALUABLES SECONDS OF SELF
...........REPEAT,GIVES PRACTICE

✦ ✦ ✦

THE BRIDGE I GAVE YOU 2 CROSS,
ONLY TAKE A SECOND 2 CROSS................SELF

✦ ✦ ✦

COME 2 MY WORLD OF JOY,
IT WILL EASE THE WORLD OF ANGER.................SELF

✦ ✦ ✦

LOVE MY SELF,
RESPECT MY SELF,
VALUE MY SELF,
PUT THESE IN THE MIRROR
OF YOUR HEART DURING THE DAY

❖ ❖ ❖

THE FUTURE IS ONLY A SECOND AWAYS

❖ ❖ ❖

THE PAST IS OUR FUTURE,
THAT JUS WHEN BY
A SECOND AGO

❖ ❖ ❖

BLESS IS THE SECONDS
THAT GIVES YOU, UNDERSTANDING

❖ ❖ ❖

ATTACH YOUR SELF TO SELF ,
CAUSE THAT THE IN NEED IS
GOING TO HELP US
WHEN THE CHIP ARE DOWN

❖ ❖ ❖

Angel Ramos

COME TO MY PATH,
SO I CAN TEACH
YOU THE LIGHT IN SELF

✦ ✦ ✦

IF YOU BE MY FOUNDATION,
I WILL BE YOUR BLESS

✦ ✦ ✦

COMES SHINE ON ME,
SO I CAN BE YOUR SMILE
WHY IS IT ME THAT YOU SEE,
I AM YOU THAT YOU NEEED!!!!!
………………..SELF

✦ ✦ ✦

THE WORLD IN ONE
SEEN WITH THESE SECONDS….
IF THE WORLD KNOW
HOW 2 READ CANDLE
EVEN SMALL ONES
LIKE THESE WORD.
THEY ARE THE PATH OF WALKS

✦ ✦ ✦

its time 4 me 2 let my mind do the thinking.

while i do my understanding
in this freezing second of the days............................
what would i do 4 a
klondike bar NOW, STAY HOME
SELF VANITY................

✦ ✦ ✦

cold is always
in the freezing weather,
never in the warm heart
COMING IN 2 A SORROUNDING,
WHERE THE DARKNESS RULES.
BUT THE LIGHT CONQUER................................SELF

✦ ✦ ✦

SADNESS IS A HOLIDAY TRADITIONS, IT PHAZESSSSSSS

✦ ✦ ✦

WHEN MY MIND GOES BONKER,
THE UNDERSTANDIN SAY RELAX

✦ ✦ ✦

INSIDE YOU CAN DISCOVER TO SELF,
THE ABILITY OF UNDERSTANDING,
THINKING, FAITH IN SELF.
EVERYTHING IS IN THERE

Angel Ramos

LOVE, RESPECT, VALUE, TRUTH,
REALITY, COMPASION, WILL,
STRENGTH, POWER., LIGHT, BLESSIN, TRIUMPH, .
THIS IS A PIECE OF THE TRUE ACTIONS.................
IT FREE AND REWARDING..........IN SELF

✦ ✦ ✦

wondering wHat the wonders of the mind do.
 oh yeahhhhhhhhhh..........JUS THINK, WOW....................SELF
SEARCH IN THE INNER SKY
THAT IS IN YOUR HEART,
THE WINDS CARRY WORDS
THAT MAKES YOUR HEART
SHINE IN DARKEN TIMES.......................SELF

✦ ✦ ✦

UNDERSTANDING KNOWS EVERYTHING,
KNOWLEDGE KNOWS THAT!!!!!!!!!!!................SELF

✦ ✦ ✦

THE WORLD IS IN YOU,
THAT YOUR HEART POSSES

✦ ✦ ✦

I AM NOT SMARTER THAN A FIFTH GRADER,
BUT WISER THAN A PHILOSOPHER.............................SELF

✦ ✦ ✦

CAN YOU CATCH WAT UNDERNEATH YOU,
OR IN TOP OF IT'S CALLED THE CORAZON...........................
SELF GIFT

✦ ✦ ✦

i come 2 be what you are WORDS.........................SELF
IF WE SHOVEL ALL
THAT DARKNESS WE HAVE,
YOU WILL SEE IS NICE
AND CLEAN THE LIGHT IN SELF
UNDERSTANDING IS THE SHOVEL

✦ ✦ ✦

YOU MIGHT SEE A MOUNTAIN,
BUT IT REALLY A PARTICLE
DON'T COVER YOUR LIGHT WITH INCIDENTS,
LET THE LIGHT COMFORT YOUR INCIDENTS
SO YOUR SECONDS MAY BE FILL WITH JOY

✦ ✦ ✦

communicatios is a friend,
relations is a friend.
A HUG IS A FRIEND!!!

✦ ✦ ✦

Angel Ramos

LOOKING AT THE WORDS SELF,
GIVE YOU THE PATH OF VIEWING
LET ME COME 2 YOU,
SO I CAN COVER ALL
THE DARKNESS THAT YOU ARE.
WITH THE LITTLE SHADE THAT I AM
........................BELIEVE

✦ ✦ ✦

COME WALK ON NOTHING,
YOU CAN STEP ON EVERYTHING.
SO YOU CAN SEE THE PATH
OF SOMETHING THAT IN SELF..............
THE PATH IS THINKING OF UNDERSTANDING

✦ ✦ ✦

CANDLES, MATCHES, FIRE, LIGHT,
CONCEPTS OF THE INNER SELF.........

✦ ✦ ✦

BITES THE WORDS,
SO YOU UNDERSTANDING
THE TASTES IN SELF....

✦ ✦ ✦

DESCISIONS, DETERMINED, DESTINATIONS

..............................AWARENESS
I AM THE MIRROR
......................SELF

✦ ✦ ✦

AS YOU TURN THE PEBBLE,
THE HERIZON BRIGHTEN
..............................SELF

✦ ✦ ✦

SMILING GIVE SENCE OF HUMOR,
WHICH IT BUILDS SELF UNDERSTANDING
OF HOW THE MOMENTS ARE AWESOME

✦ ✦ ✦

TO COMMUNICATE WTH MY ESSENCE,
YOU MUST VISION MY WORDS .....

✦ ✦ ✦

BEIN MY BLESS,
YOU MUST BE MY SECONDS

✦ ✦ ✦

CARRY YOUR TEARS,
DON'T DRIED THEM

HOW CAN YOU WALK ON THE MATTER,
WHEN UNDERSTANDING IS DOING THE STEPPING

✦ ✦ ✦

IN THIS UNIVERSE THERE IS A ELEMENT CALLED SELF,
THAT IS THE PARTICLE OF EVERYTHING IN SELF

✦ ✦ ✦

be the steps that be yr walk,
not the walk that be yr step
AS THE BRAIN EZZZZZZZZZZ,
IS COMFORT THE STRENGTH.

✦ ✦ ✦

IF YOU PRESS 2 FINGER 2GETHER,
THAT IS TRUE THE SIZE OF ANY CONFLICT

✦ ✦ ✦

GO INTO THE INNER MOST,
SO YOU CAN REACH THE OUTTER MOST..............

✦ ✦ ✦

MAY THE NEW HERIZON, BRING YOU VISONS,,,,,,,,,,,

BECOME THE WORD,
THAT YOU TRUELY ARE SELF,
GUESS WHAT AND WILL ALWAYS BE

✦ ✦ ✦

WHY WE MAKE LIFE
AS SMALL AS A PARTICLE,
WHEN IT'S BIGGER
THAN YOU CAN IMAGINE
...............................SELF

✦ ✦ ✦

tears TAMES THE SMILES,
2 IT'S GREATNESS...........................SELF

✦ ✦ ✦

IN THIS UNIVERSE THERE IS
A ELEMENT CALLED SELF,
THAT IS THE PARTICLE
OF EVERYTHING IN SELF

✦ ✦ ✦

BITES THE WORDS,
SO YOU UNDERSTANDING
THE TASTES IN SELF

I SEE EVERYTHING
THAT WAS NOTHING BEFORE
...................SELF

♦ ♦ ♦

visions THE BREATH
OF YOUR WORDS,
THAN YOU CAN CLAIM THE WALK
IN YOUR STEP IN UNDERSTANDING..SELF

♦ ♦ ♦

GRAB YOUR VISIONS,
SO YOU CAN BE THE TRUTH LOOK
..........................self

♦ ♦ ♦

VISIONS YOUR WORDS,
AS THE WAVES
ARE ON THE SHORE ......
REPEATLY SO FOCUS
APPEAR ON YOU AS
MUCH AS YOU CAN.
SO YOU CAN BE ON
YOUR AWARENESS
ON UNDERSTANDING.
SO YOU BECOME
THE PRESENT OF YOU....................SELF
A SIMPLE WORD CAN

EMPOWER YOUR PATH

✦ ✦ ✦

WORDS CAN WALK,
WORDS CAN REACH.
WORDS CAN BECOME YOU
………………….SELF

✦ ✦ ✦

STEP INTO THE DAYS,
SO YOU CAN RELAX INTO THE NIGHT
……………SELF IN SECONDS

✦ ✦ ✦

WHY ASK WHEN YOU DONT NEEDS,
YOU JUS WANT I DONT HAVE WANT.
I CAN ONLY PROVIDE NEEDS.
I WISH I COULD BUT IN TRUE
REALITY IN THE TRUTH OF UNDERSTANDING
I LIVE IN NEEDS I DONT LIKE
THE WANTS TO BELIEVE IN
THE PRESENTS OF THE TRUE WORDS

✦ ✦ ✦

IF UNDERSTANDING QUESTION THINKING
PLEASE HAVE A ANOTHER BULB READY……..

Angel Ramos

i jus needs words that i need,
not words that i want.................self

♦ ♦ ♦

when lost in words,
be found in understanding
.................self

♦ ♦ ♦

tears are to refresh the visions of words,
so we may answer the why in understanding......................self

♦ ♦ ♦

why we look at understanding as assumptions,
when it's the reality in.............self

♦ ♦ ♦

opinions is like a joy
stick anybody can play with it.
understanding is the truth,
something you can play with.

♦ ♦ ♦

COME 2 MY REACH,
SO I CAN BECOME

YOUR DISTANCE................SELF
I AM YR DISTANCE,
AS YOU ARE MY REACH
..................I AM, I AM

♦ ♦ ♦

BECOME MY STEP,
SO YOU CAN BE THE CLOUDS
.................SELF

♦ ♦ ♦

SIMPLE RESOLVED COMPLEX,
COMPLEX CAN'T RESOLVED SIMPLE....

♦ ♦ ♦

TRAIN MY WORDS WITH PRACTICE,
AND YOU WILL BE THE VISIONS OF UNDERSTANDING
...................INNER SELF

♦ ♦ ♦

TO SEE HOW HISTORY CAN SAVE THE FUTURE,
YOU MUST BECOME THE PRESENTS
..............BELIEVE TO THE BELIEVERS

♦ ♦ ♦

Angel Ramos

GIVE ME A WORD, I'LL GIVE YOU A FUTURE,
GIVE ME AN EMOTIONS, I'LL GIVE YOU HISTORY
...................................UNDERSTANDING
to see the emotions
in the clouds,
visions the rain
in the words........................self

✦ ✦ ✦

the wealth of the WORDS,
is the expirience that's
felt in the understanding..................self

✦ ✦ ✦

carry your faith in words,
so you second become your blessing...............self

✦ ✦ ✦

ROADS, PATHS, TRAILS,
DON'T MATTER JUS SEEK
................................SELF

✦ ✦ ✦

COME BE MY WORDS,
SO I CAN BECOME
YOUR SPIRITS..................SELF

WORDS OF THE LORD
IS THE UNDERSTANDING OF SELF,
WHICH GIVE US
THE FOOT PRINTS OF LIFE.
IT SHINE THE PATH
TO THE KINGDOM OF HEAVEN
....
SELF UNDERSTANDING AND BELIEVING

✦ ✦ ✦

WITH PRACTICE YOU CAN
RIDE A BIKE OR A HORSE.
WITH PRACTICE YOU CAN FIND
UNDERSTANDING IN WORDS,
NOT THERE MEANING....................SELF

✦ ✦ ✦

if two reaches become as one,
guess what there it is,,,,,,,,,,,,,self

✦ ✦ ✦

two mountains can become one grain,
with the love of sweet understanding

✦ ✦ ✦

two pillars of faith can become one blessing

Angel Ramos

become my marathon walker,
so i can become youe water dispatcher.............self

♦ ♦ ♦

with two maps,
we could become one road.

♦ ♦ ♦

a pearl only can be seen
if light is given.................self

♦ ♦ ♦

PRONOUNCE THE WORD LOVE SLOWLY,
LISTEN TO THE SOUND. NOW TELL
YOURSELF IS THAT THE TRUTH
.....................................SELF

♦ ♦ ♦

WALK IN THE PATH OF UNDERSTANDING,
SO YOU CAN HEAR THE ECHO OF THE PRESENTS
......................SELF

♦ ♦ ♦

PAINT A PICTURE OF A WORDS IN SELF,
NOW YOU JUST BECAME PART OF UNDERSTANDING

..................................SELF

IF I LOOK AT YOU UNDERSTANDING,
WHY CAN'T I READ YOU.
MAYBE I SHOULD VISIONS YOU,
AND HEAR YOU. SO I CAN
BECOME WHAT YOU ARE..................SELF

✦ ✦ ✦

WHY I GIVE YOU MY WORDS AS UNDERSTANDING,
AND YOU RECIEVE THEM AS EMOTIONS.........................SELF

✦ ✦ ✦

IF I SEND MY TEARS TO RESCUE YOU,
WHY YOU USE THEM TO SINK YOUR SELF
....................................WORDS OF RESCUE

✦ ✦ ✦

COME CLIMB THE MOUNTAINS OF YOUR TEARS,
SO YOU CAN SEE IS ONLY A DROP............................SELF

✦ ✦ ✦

WHY FIGHT SELF,
WHEN YOU SHOULD
BE HUGGIN SELF................
THE SIMPLE AND

COMPLEX IN SELF
ACTING IS FOR THE SCREEM,
BECOMING IS FOR YOU...............
SELF UNDERSTANDING

♦ ♦ ♦

BECOMES A CHOIR ,
BALANCE THE BTFUL
SOUNDS OF WORDS IN SELF.
AND HEAR THE BEAUTY
OF UNDERSTANDING.............SELF

♦ ♦ ♦

IF WORDS CAN FOLLOW A PATH,
WHY CAN'T YOU BE THE ROUTE.
.................WALLS OF EMOTIONS

♦ ♦ ♦

MAY second BE BLESS WITH
THE STRENGTH OF UNITY

♦ ♦ ♦

TEARS SAY HELP ME,
UNITY SAYS I'M HERE....

♦ ♦ ♦

MAY ----- AMAZING GRACE -----
BE THE FOUNDATIONS FOR seconds

TEARS SAY HELP ME,
UNITY SAYS I'M HERE....

✦ ✦ ✦

SELF FEEL ASHAME ASKING THIS
-----PLEASE, PLEASE, PLEASE-----
LET'S BE UNDERSTANDING,
SO THE BONDING BECOMES A UNITY

✦ ✦ ✦

it's a shame catastrophe
can see unity, BUT WAR CAN'T....

✦ ✦ ✦

a penny can be a faith,
a dollar will be the blessin...

✦ ✦ ✦

blind is the eyes that don't touch
.................BLESS PRESENT !!!

✦ ✦ ✦

PUT YOUR SWORD DOWN AND HELP...........................SELF

✦ ✦ ✦

GIVE ME YOUR WORDS THAT I GIVE....
WORDS THAT GUIDE,
HEART THAT SEE...

✦ ✦ ✦

VISIONNIG THE UNDERSTANDING,
FREE THE PAIN.....

✦ ✦ ✦

BUILD YOUR WORDS,
SO YOU CAN WALK YOUR PATH.....

✦ ✦ ✦

GIVE A BLESSIN WITH UNDERSTANDING,
YOU WILL GET A SMILE SEAL WITH FAITH,

✦ ✦ ✦

DAYS ARE SHORTER THAN SECOND,
IF YOU LOOK IN THE FUTURE...............PRESENTS SAYS.

✦ ✦ ✦

DON'T WAIT ON THE DAY, REMEMBER A SECONDS ALWAYS COME 1ST

✦ ✦ ✦

A YEAR FROM NOW,
WOULD BE NOW

where the wind roar,
the water ease.................
understanding thy emotions

✦ ✦ ✦

when your emotions start bitting,
tame them with your understanding.
so the blessin clear it path............................self

✦ ✦ ✦

YOUR ARM CAN HUG A MOUNTAINS....................SELF

✦ ✦ ✦

YOUR ARMS THE MEDICINE 4 SECOND
........................INNER REACH IN WORD

✦ ✦ ✦

AN UNDERSTANDING HEART
CAN SAVE CRYING ARMS

✦ ✦ ✦

SECOND IS PLAYING A TUNE,
IT'S OUR DUTY TO LISTEN 2 TO THE SOUND

✦ ✦ ✦

CARRY THE LENGTH OF PRESENT,
BY THE REACHES OF THY HEART

✦ ✦ ✦

HELP, HELP, AND HELP================
UNDERSTANDING.............REWARD IS FINDING

✦ ✦ ✦

UNDERSTANDING, START CURRENTS OF THINKIN

✦ ✦ ✦

CARRY THE TEARS WITH UNDERSTANDING, NOT EMOTIONS.
SO YOUR ARMS MAY EXTEND IN SECONDS PRESENT

✦ ✦ ✦

ESSENCE IS THE GROUND
ZERO OF UNDERSTANDING
....................PLEASE REACH.

♦ ♦ ♦

A MYTH IS A SUBSTANCE OF UNDERSTANDING.
A THEORY IS A PATTERN OF THINKING.
A ESSENCE IS REALITY OF LOVE……..

♦ ♦ ♦

ESSENCE, DIVINE, SPIRIT, UNDERSTANDING, SELF
.............................A PLATE OF FOOD
THE ENTERPRISE IN SELF,
IS THE SEARCH FOR PRAISE......................
THE UNITY OF COMPLEX IN SIMPLE

♦ ♦ ♦

WITH THE MIX-TER OF SIMPLE,
AND THE COMPLEX OF WATER,
WE HAVE A JELLO OF AN UNDERSTANDING...........................
SELF

♦ ♦ ♦

SEE NOTHING,
VISIONS EVERYTHING,
WITH THE SOMETHING

CALL UNDERSTANDING..................
THE EXPIRIENCE OF SELF IS EVERY NOW

✦ ✦ ✦

ONLY UNDERSTANDING OF THE THINKING.
CAN BRING YOU TO THE DISTANCE
OF UNDERSTANDING OF CLOSE-NESS...............SELF

✦ ✦ ✦

EDUCATIONS IS THE UNDERSTANDING OF WHAT IS
.............................SELF COMPLETE AWARENESS

✦ ✦ ✦

COMPLETE YOUR BOUNDERIES,
SO YOU BECOME THE GOAL
....................WORDS WITH DEFINE

✦ ✦ ✦

BECOME THE WORDS
THAT ARE FLOW-ING,
SO YOU BECOME THE PERSON
THAT WALK THE TALK....................
INNER UNDERSTANDING
OF TRUE BEING

✦ ✦ ✦

HOW CAN YOU STRENGHTEN THE SILENT,
WHEN YOUR NOW IS EMPTY..............
THE PRESENTS BRING THE NOW

✦ ✦ ✦

DON'T GET TIRED OF THY WORDS,
BE THE STRENGTH OF THY WORDS
...........THE WINGS OF WORDS

✦ ✦ ✦

PLACE ME YOUR PATHS,
AND YOU WILL REACH MY ABILITY
........................SELF THY SELF
POWER IS NOTHING,
iF YOU BELIEVE IN SOMETHING,
POWER HAS EVERYTHING,
IF YOU SEE THE STILLNESS
IN MOVEMENT...............
INNER CREATIONS

✦ ✦ ✦

AS WE SEEK, THE EFFORD PRESENTS.................SELF

✦ ✦ ✦

BECOME THE SECOND,
IN A HOUR YOU WILL BE THE SAME.................YOU

♦ ♦ ♦

THE THEORY OF ---- WHAT --- IS IN AM

♦ ♦ ♦

AS WE SEARCH IN THE DEPTH OF HONEST,
A PEARL WILL BE FOUND..........................UNDERSTANDING

♦ ♦ ♦

GIFTS COME IN SOUND,
IF YOU READ THE PITCH IN THE TUNE
......................INNER NOISE
BE THE FORTUNE OF YOUR TELLING
.............................SELF

♦ ♦ ♦

BE THE INNER LISTENER,
USE YOUR HEART AS THE MIC
...................SELF INNER SENSE

♦ ♦ ♦

AS WORDS FALL,
AS LACK OF MEANNING.
INNER UNDERSTANDING
GIVES IT LIFT,
WINGS THAT CAN'T BE SEEN

AS THE STRENGTH OF SOUND..................SELF

♦ ♦ ♦

tears spell understanding,
pain spell darkness,
and you spell HELP!!!!

♦ ♦ ♦

I WILL WALK ANY DISTANCE
2 BOND 2 YOUR WORDS
...................SELF

THE LENGTH OF THE UNIVERSE IS ONLY A SECOND,
WHEN I HEAR YOURS WORDS
.........................INNER LECTURES

♦ ♦ ♦

THE SOUNDS OF WORDS,
S THE FORCE OF MY WILL
............UNDERSTANDING SOUND

♦ ♦ ♦

HEAR ME, THAT WAY WE CAN WALK 2GETHER
....................FOOT MARKS.

♦ ♦ ♦

THE KEY 2 MY TEMPLE IS UNDERSTANDING,
WHICH OPEN ANY DOOR.
THAT NEEDS 2 OPEN ITS HERIZON

✦ ✦ ✦

BREAK WALLS WITH SOUND..........................LISTEN

✦ ✦ ✦

CATCH THE DISTANCE WITH
ONE VISIONS CALLED ABILITY.
.......................AWARENESS.
HERIZON IS CATCHING SELF,
AND YOU BEIN THE SUNNNN

✦ ✦ ✦

ACCOMPLISMENT ARE THE WORDS IN SELF,
REWARDS ARE WORDS IN SELF,
RELATIONS ARE WORDS IN SELF,
UNDERSTANDING ARE WORDS IN SELF.
.......................WORDS OF THY SELF OR _____.....

✦ ✦ ✦

BE MY FRIEND,
AIN'T ASHAMED OF ASKING
...................SELF

✦ ✦ ✦

LET ME CARRY YOUR ATTITUDE,
SO YOU BECOME MY PEACE........................SELF

✦ ✦ ✦

hollow be thy name,
under that is thy self
..............understanding thy self...
as i walk in..............awareness of understanding self

✦ ✦ ✦

i will fear no...........................
strenght in believe in self

✦ ✦ ✦

i am the words of your enlightment......................self

✦ ✦ ✦

a word is empty until i give them
strength by understanding..............walkin paths

✦ ✦ ✦

WHY?---- DON'T ANSWER THE QUESTIONS,
AND YOU HAVE YOUR ANSWER........................SELF

♦ ♦ ♦

SEE WHAT'S NOT THERE,
GUESS WHAT BELIEVE ME
 IT'S REALLY THERE.......................SELF

♦ ♦ ♦

VISIONS HAVE EYES CALLED WORDS
..............................SELF

WHAT IS THE BAIT FOR A TRUE FISHER, SELF
................UNDERSTANDING

♦ ♦ ♦

IF RAIN GIVE LIFE,
WHAT UNDERSTANDING
WORDS GIVE................REBIRTH

♦ ♦ ♦

HOW I WONDER--------------
THE LONG DISTANCE
OF SHORT MEMORY....................
THE WHAT THE blank IN SELF,

♦ ♦ ♦

BLESS, FAITH, SUCH Out-WER
WORDS WITH NO FOUNDATIONS.................SELF

✦ ✦ ✦

PORKIN YOUR SELF WITH A FORK,
IS LIKE MARINATING EMOTIONS.
...........SELF INTERESTS

✦ ✦ ✦

REACHING FOR WORDS TO BE IN THE PRESENTS
.......................ENLIGHTMENT OF NOW

PRESENT HAS A DREAM, MAY I SAYS THIS WITH
UNDERSTANDING TEARS. THAT DREAM IS YOU.....

✦ ✦ ✦

DON'T BE THE EXAMPLE OF THE PRODUCT,
BE THE PRODUCT.................SELF

✦ ✦ ✦

BECOME THE DISTANCE
OF YOUR PAST,
SO YOU WILL BECOME
THE REACH OF YOU FUTURE...................
THE ARMS OF REACH IS UNDERSTANDING
THE PRESENTS IN SELF

♦ ♦ ♦

REACHING FOR WORDS
TO BE IN THE PRESENT
........ENLIGHTMENT OF NOW

♦ ♦ ♦

THE EXPLANATIONS OF EVERYTHING
IS THE QUESTIONS OF ANSWER IN SELF

♦ ♦ ♦

THE SUM OF NOTHING IS IN THE
UNDERSTANDING AND THINKING IN SELF
UNDERSTANDING THE ANSWER,
IS TO QUESTION THE THINKING.................SELF

♦ ♦ ♦

UNDERSTANDING IS THE
BIGGEST THING IN NOTHING
.................SELF

♦ ♦ ♦

FRAGILE AS AIR,
STRONG AS WIND
.................WORDS IN SELF

✦ ✦ ✦

ZENDA IS THE NIRVANA IN BUDDA,
WHEN CONFUCIUS SEE THE GURU IN SELF
................................UNDERSTANDING

✦ ✦ ✦

One don't measure a smile by a sentence, it measures with hugs

✦ ✦ ✦

Love, the first-aid kit of words

✦ ✦ ✦

If you teach your words to smile
The mirror will laugh joyfully...

✦ ✦ ✦

Have one ever play in word, As how to be self....

✦ ✦ ✦

The parent of the child Is the sentence of the word

✦ ✦ ✦

How to clear the mirror, just smile

Angel Ramos

✦ ✦ ✦

Once a sentence told a word HI, the end

✦ ✦ ✦

Sound, the glasses of the eyes

✦ ✦ ✦

The repeated words called mirror

✦ ✦ ✦

Label the sentence, Become the word of a smile

✦ ✦ ✦

Simple, simple, simple, funny three second of simple…… let that sink in

✦ ✦ ✦

Smile is the puzzle of the laugh
Smile the spoon of food for thought

✦ ✦ ✦

The spirit of your shadow, is the guidance of present

✦ ✦ ✦

Light of essence
Tabloids of billboard
The laugh in the smile
Or the words in self

✦ ✦ ✦

Light the stepping stone smile, with its rite sentence

✦ ✦ ✦

Love the word that pick up spirit with its understanding

✦ ✦ ✦

The circle in the word

✦ ✦ ✦

The parallel in the line

✦ ✦ ✦

In the secret of a library
Stand out a sentence as a word

✦ ✦ ✦

The sentence is the follower of the words
 And the paragraph is the smile of the chapter

Angel Ramos

✦ ✦ ✦

Present as see is view

✦ ✦ ✦

Present, the always
For I am is always now

✦ ✦ ✦

The two beginning of self is, I am

✦ ✦ ✦

You can mobile a sentence,
JUS BE THE CONDUCTOR OF A WORD

✦ ✦ ✦

DEEP IN THE FOREST, a drop is heard

✦ ✦ ✦

Once upon a time,
a word ask a sentence.
HEY ARE YOU SAYING THE TRUTH
the end.... Sincerely PRESENT

✦ ✦ ✦

Is darker in NO-SITE
THE HEARING OF NOTHING
A VOICE CAN DRAW

✦ ✦ ✦

Word fit better in human,
than SHE or He.
The wall of voice

✦ ✦ ✦

NOW is the billboard of a word

✦ ✦ ✦

The moment is the sentence of a smile

✦ ✦ ✦

Draw present be a word in now

✦ ✦ ✦

Smile the painted mirror

✦ ✦ ✦

The dot of life, PRESENT

Angel Ramos

❖ ❖ ❖

Present, silence beginning.

❖ ❖ ❖

I see nothing, the start-kit
Remember one can see nothing
Everything center-Ness
Silent painted voice

❖ ❖ ❖

You can label essence, jus smile
The point is the sentence

❖ ❖ ❖

Laugh it's a easy JOB..

❖ ❖ ❖

The MINE of a word its it story

❖ ❖ ❖

Scrabble and science, what is a sentence of a word

❖ ❖ ❖

May the love in one
Be present as essence

❦ ❦ ❦

Write on one perform, a smile

❦ ❦ ❦

The word action as motion in movement

❦ ❦ ❦

Read as one read essence

❦ ❦ ❦

Un-weave the understanding
As one un-twine the thinking
The puzzle of a word
Is the maze of its sentence
Complex simple is perplex

❦ ❦ ❦

I am the true, words of understanding
But as a sentence, I present thy AM

❦ ❦ ❦

Angel Ramos

Understanding, the true book of thinking
A bunch of sand in a hand
Are the words of a book
The btful day at the beach !!
To be love in self Is 2 love the word
The thousand word of a picture is @M
Can you say, who's in present. .... I AM
Once upon time before thinking,
there was understanding.
The end was told as truth of told.
Said say as spoken,
the where of how is IS

✦ ✦ ✦

   Self as essence Name,
the words Last name,
it's sentence
Part of being before the label
Love in understanding
The art of thinking

✦ ✦ ✦

The echo in the voice
Quiet of the silence

A word as a ✦ ✦ ✦

✦ ✦ ✦

Thinking voice is understanding
Essence movement,
Love action
As a sentence walks
A word reach for hugs
Together understanding LIFE

✦ ✦ ✦

The candle of a sentence
Is the lit words of understanding

✦ ✦ ✦

Be essence as understanding

✦ ✦ ✦

The inscription of love
Is a word as a sentence

✦ ✦ ✦

As simple start
END understand
The story of a word
Is the sentence of understanding

Angel Ramos

✦ ✦ ✦

A word, the voice of essence

✦ ✦ ✦

Download a sentence
To delete the tears of words

✦ ✦ ✦

Paragraph a smile
To label the word

✦ ✦ ✦

A sentence is the eye
As the word is the essence

✦ ✦ ✦

The open door-window
is the word of the smile in the heart

✦ ✦ ✦

Just like the earth
Not seen in the universe
The word not seem in essence
But in sentence

All is seen in book
The created SELF..

♦ ♦ ♦

Essence is the universe
Understanding is the world
Thinking are the people
Love are the smile
Movements are the action
The art of words

♦ ♦ ♦

Love sign every smile
Jus become it's proper word

♦ ♦ ♦

Sound like action
But is drawn in movement
The essence as art
But live in words

♦ ♦ ♦

You carry the truth,
the literature of understanding

♦ ♦ ♦

Angel Ramos

Make a word, the pillar of its understanding

✦ ✦ ✦

Sentence, the action of a word

✦ ✦ ✦

Smiles the only guidance of essence

✦ ✦ ✦

Thinking cover,
the essence of understanding

✦ ✦ ✦

Smile, the pen of life
Space the page of essence

✦ ✦ ✦

Be a while of NOW...

✦ ✦ ✦

Smile, the origin of present

✦ ✦ ✦

Think-tank
Mirror of understanding

✦ ✦ ✦

Magic, how to hear words of silence

✦ ✦ ✦

When why is who's NOW
Is to be where in was words present

✦ ✦ ✦

I am the motion of understanding
Call the action of thinking
Essence as a sentence of words

✦ ✦ ✦

Nothing the creation of words
I am the cement of building
I am the words

✦ ✦ ✦

Browsing words makes understanding
The lego of thinking...

✦ ✦ ✦

Angel Ramos

As present describe ESSENCE
UNDERSTANDING pages thinking

♦ ♦ ♦

A sentence of a word

♦ ♦ ♦

Is the thinking of understanding

♦ ♦ ♦

Page, a sentence as a WORD

♦ ♦ ♦

A word is the stepping- ladder of a sentence

♦ ♦ ♦

A star is not a bright light, but a firm smile

♦ ♦ ♦

Post a statement, be the RELIC..

♦ ♦ ♦

Like the story of the scripture,

essence as understanding...

✦ ✦ ✦

Don't let it rain beneath one HAIR
AM, part of the words
that complete the whole sentence....

✦ ✦ ✦

Love is the shield,
and understanding is the sword.

✦ ✦ ✦

Love, the two thing of one is I AM

✦ ✦ ✦

Present, the sentence of AM

✦ ✦ ✦

Focus, the stillness of IS..

✦ ✦ ✦

Existence as told
Exist as explain
The words as truth

Angel Ramos

The essence as experience
ONLY words MOVE

❖ ❖ ❖

Love solid as water
Tears silence as smile

❖ ❖ ❖

Silence the book of nothing,
but yet tell all in told.
Say as see,
the engrave of sentence
rock words

❖ ❖ ❖

Thinking has a language,
that only understanding can read it's silence

❖ ❖ ❖

Thought as an atom
An atom as a decision
Essence the instructor of thinking
as understanding

❖ ❖ ❖

Forgive for the word don't know
Understanding the teacher as thinking

✦ ✦ ✦

Love travel in a sentence,
　the products of words

✦ ✦ ✦

A reflection is a word,
in its mirror is the smile.

✦ ✦ ✦

The guardian as a sentence
The angel as a word
The essence as experience
And the UNDERSTANDING as being
How to become, a smile in PRESENT

✦ ✦ ✦

Favoring the best,
looking at mirror

✦ ✦ ✦

The call of wind or wings is a sentence

Angel Ramos

✦ ✦ ✦

Seeing is when view hear

✦ ✦ ✦

One is ability truth in essence

✦ ✦ ✦

One is the basic of a sound,
the simple Word

✦ ✦ ✦

Circle, the straight WORD sentence

✦ ✦ ✦

IS as BE in a sentence

✦ ✦ ✦

The better-half of a sentence
Is the complete of the decision

✦ ✦ ✦

The way to a big WORD,
can be a small sentence.

Xample:: WHY is a small sentence.
Understanding, the gravity of a sentence

✦ ✦ ✦

One can get 60 second in minute
But one get a whole smile in one-second

✦ ✦ ✦

Less-more the balance of simple

✦ ✦ ✦

A bucket of a ocean
A tear of a hand...

✦ ✦ ✦

A word as a leader
is a step in decision

✦ ✦ ✦

Hug one-self and feel the value of a smile

✦ ✦ ✦

Nothing is the pen of something
that creates everything......

Angel Ramos

♦ ♦ ♦

Decision can polish a mirror, just smile

♦ ♦ ♦

How to use a sentence in a word
define a mirror

♦ ♦ ♦

Silent is the language of essence....
understanding prints thinking, as writing in view

♦ ♦ ♦

If one look at a word it has reading
essence writing as understanding...

♦ ♦ ♦

The curator of a smile,
is a word.
A sentence is its shine

♦ ♦ ♦

The conductor of a pilots
is the heart not the finger...
 the lite note

✦ ✦ ✦

Paint me above,
and see the art below....
Inner-being of words

✦ ✦ ✦

A heart can read the sky of a word...

✦ ✦ ✦

Reason meaning is understanding think...
a word written as a sentence of guidance

✦ ✦ ✦

If one give a view,
I will stand below to vision...
Said, the secret words

✦ ✦ ✦

Words are the walker of essence...
movement action called understanding...

✦ ✦ ✦

Silent and quietness
sound are words,

the life in essence...

✦ ✦ ✦

Understanding, the silent language of essence

✦ ✦ ✦

The water-fall, and the wind in trees both sing.
Sound of beauty nature, essence harmony of love.
Sharing language silent of IS.

✦ ✦ ✦

The fashion of words is love,
just smile and watch
the garden of light appear....

✦ ✦ ✦

Love is simple as a smile,
jus read the word one gave it

✦ ✦ ✦

Understanding, the silent language of essence

✦ ✦ ✦

The world has a branch call the sentence..

✦ ✦ ✦

One can touch a smile
If the heart is the hand...

✦ ✦ ✦

A tear is more solid than water,
a wall of a sentence

✦ ✦ ✦

Essence as simple
is understanding that thinking THINK

✦ ✦ ✦

Essence circle straight line
is a words sentence

✦ ✦ ✦

Essence is how understanding Tutor thinking....
a word movement in silence
is painting an art in as a sentence

✦ ✦ ✦

The link of word
is the

Angel Ramos

✦ ✦ ✦

...

✦ ✦ ✦

Yours, mine, and truth is the decision of thought as essence...

✦ ✦ ✦

3 double is one word
Seek the saw in see,
jus view words in thought.
And decision quest as smile

✦ ✦ ✦

Hate can be a smile in knowing self....
tricks of trade.. don't let custom or tradition RULED...
become the custom of thy tradition jus smile

✦ ✦ ✦

Only the sentence
is the light of a smile word

✦ ✦ ✦

Nothing Is simple,
not walls....

✦ ✦ ✦

Dare one to write on NOTHInG,
but use a smile

✦ ✦ ✦

HEARTS, the wifi of words,,,

✦ ✦ ✦

A smile wall
is like scent of a word..

✦ ✦ ✦

A sentence has 2 column of 1,
the SMILE and the TEAR
Twice-A-light,
sound of a sentence......

✦ ✦ ✦

SAY, the word in IS

✦ ✦ ✦

One can carve words
But that don't reason
With the thinking understanding...

The answer to question
Is to ASK

♦ ♦ ♦

♦ ♦ ♦

The window to sound
Is to hear the told…..

♦ ♦ ♦

AM, the mirror of echoes as I

♦ ♦ ♦

Essence is MIRROR Understanding
is REFLECTION THINKING is echoes

♦ ♦ ♦

Let the echoes be the mirror of reflection

♦ ♦ ♦

A mirror has a sentence in one word…..SELF
If everything shine

Why add paint....
The instructed smile

♦ ♦ ♦

The particle of a smile
are the requested words of the heart

♦ ♦ ♦

The parallel of a paragraph are it's WORDS

♦ ♦ ♦

When what question why,
AM became a mirror

♦ ♦ ♦

Time don't have periods and question,
it only has the AM and I as SELF

♦ ♦ ♦

Travel in time, as a ruler

♦ ♦ ♦

The ART of mist, the laugh

Angel Ramos

✦ ✦ ✦

Let me read
your silence
Said a decision
To a thought

✦ ✦ ✦

The beginning of start
Is to END....

✦ ✦ ✦

The origin of LIFE
Is a SMILE.....

✦ ✦ ✦

STRONG, the words in duty

✦ ✦ ✦

Once upon a present.
There live told as heard…

✦ ✦ ✦

Don't give the present a sentence,
give a smile

ART-FUL SMILES

✦ ✦ ✦

WILL shadow is DUTY
WHY ESSENCE is AM
WHO UNDERSTANDING is I

✦ ✦ ✦

What better dream,
but to understand words

✦ ✦ ✦

INTEL, the sentence of a DREAM...

✦ ✦ ✦

UNDERSTANDING smiles
as THINKING become it's mirror

✦ ✦ ✦

Before the 1st thought,
understanding deliver.
The menu of words...

Angel Ramos

✦ ✦ ✦

Knowledge, how does the wheel TURN..

✦ ✦ ✦

WORDS REASON are SENTENCE

✦ ✦ ✦

Don't draw nothing
with the word of a sentence

✦ ✦ ✦

One can color white in dark....
the smile brush

✦ ✦ ✦

UNDERSTANDING, the capital of any BRIDGE...

✦ ✦ ✦

SUB-scribe, the words in UNDERSTANDING

✦ ✦ ✦

Pointing the decision,
An empty THOUGHt

Who came first the finger
Or the THOUGHT

✦ ✦ ✦

Love may yell at one,
But it's tear are sayin the truth

✦ ✦ ✦

Easy to read a book
HARD 2-stand in front of class.........
act like the class -A- BOOK!!!

✦ ✦ ✦

Circle, the understanding of CENTER

✦ ✦ ✦

Ending, the period of beginning

✦ ✦ ✦

Love sentence is a smile...
Essence written as understanding

✦ ✦ ✦

The binder of smile are words

Angel Ramos

✦ ✦ ✦

Only a smile can write tears in essence
Body-essence
Thinking-understanding
Psychology-philosophy
Love-believe
Words-being SELF-AM

✦ ✦ ✦

illusion or imagination
Thinking or understanding
Believe or creation
The EGG or chicken
A theory of the bang
The fractor of strings

✦ ✦ ✦

The page of one word is self...

✦ ✦ ✦

If one look at a drop,
one looking at life.
If one look at tear,
one looking at a story.
If one look at essence,
one looking at understanding

❖ ❖ ❖

If a sentence is a river,
then make a word a stream.
So the thought cross the decision as smile

❖ ❖ ❖

Walk the instrumental of action,
The heard in silence

❖ ❖ ❖

The shadow of a tear, is a smile..

❖ ❖ ❖

Sing in hear, the sentence of the wind

❖ ❖ ❖

Stand as IS
Love as ESSENCE

❖ ❖ ❖

Nothing the gift of freedom,
smile and see how it works...

❖ ❖ ❖

A mountain is full of nothing,
once the grain is pick.

♦ ♦ ♦

Why, be confident of nothing.

♦ ♦ ♦

Only the heart, is the definition of a smile
Mind creates
Believe deliver..

♦ ♦ ♦

Don't feed tears
Nurture SMILE
Silence story
Don't read the tear of a mirror,
it's true application is a SMILE

♦ ♦ ♦

Words are stuck to blanket

♦ ♦ ♦

Train vision movement,
words action in sound

✦ ✦ ✦

Here the view of vision,
just add a word with water

✦ ✦ ✦

Don't look nowhere,
everything beginning portion of a sentence

✦ ✦ ✦

Simple is the written, regardless

✦ ✦ ✦

The pearl of the sky
The star of the ocean
The essence of thinking
The words of understanding
Self as am in I of believe

✦ ✦ ✦

Thought, the billboard of decisions.

✦ ✦ ✦

Action is a smile
Movement are the words

Angel Ramos

✦ ✦ ✦

With a sentence
one build a bridge....
With a walk
one word it

✦ ✦ ✦

The include of words
are understanding

✦ ✦ ✦

Control is just a sentence,
not a WORD.

✦ ✦ ✦

The liquid of essence is love
the call of the wild,
hearin a word in silence
call vision

✦ ✦ ✦

Pencil and paper
As decision and though

✦ ✦ ✦

Weave the sentence as a WORD....
center-ness of thought
1st was words,
then the earth,
called the sentence

✦ ✦ ✦

There two smile,
by one balance....
study this one....
it's called center,
understanding being essence

✦ ✦ ✦

Essence as a pencil
Write and erase
Understanding and thinking

✦ ✦ ✦

Essence, the paper of a sentence.
The words of a pen,
understanding and believe....

✦ ✦ ✦

Time as space of a paper

Angel Ramos

✦ ✦ ✦

CROWN words as smile

✦ ✦ ✦

Words, the door or bridge..

✦ ✦ ✦

Jus the same way a cell-phone,
has a light app.
So does the words in understanding
Has a believe app

✦ ✦ ✦

Nothing the paper
Silence the pen
Believe the write

✦ ✦ ✦

Silence, the gifted author....

✦ ✦ ✦

Every-word has the tone of love,,,

✦ ✦ ✦

The converter,
the smile as a pen...

✦ ✦ ✦

The dungeon of darkness,
a word not heard in silence

✦ ✦ ✦

Little space to write the truth,
so I will write the truth in one WORD...
>>> LOVE <<<

✦ ✦ ✦

traveling sentence,
a walking word.
Understanding being
heard in thinking.
The essence of love
written in silence.
Hear I love
self in silence

✦ ✦ ✦

The book of silence
Is the essence of love

Angel Ramos

✦ ✦ ✦

Philosophy is read in silence
The sentence of nothing in heard

✦ ✦ ✦

Dictator, a canvas with a sentence

✦ ✦ ✦

Words, ✦ ✦ ✦

action before finger

✦ ✦ ✦

Walk with nothing,
how to write everything
with a feather

✦ ✦ ✦

Pen is the future
Pencil is the past
But the rock is the present...

✦ ✦ ✦

Only understanding can make kool-aid

✦ ✦ ✦

WHILE IS THE TIME

✦ ✦ ✦

THE SHARPER WORD
THE BLESS SENTENCE

✦ ✦ ✦

the word
the sentence
the believe
==========
ESSENCE
UNDERSTANDING
THINKING

✦ ✦ ✦

full see everything
empty see nothing
how everything read nothing
understanding essence thinking t
he cup story

✦ ✦ ✦

tears, the teacher of push-up
Smiles, the teacher of walking

✦ ✦ ✦

the fundamental of time
is the smile of joy

✦ ✦ ✦

The paint of a smile
Is the art of the laugh...
JOY of ESSENCE

✦ ✦ ✦

The fruit of truth been change,
 its not a flavor no-more.
Now is a sentence

✦ ✦ ✦

Simple, the essence...

✦ ✦ ✦

The pool of a smile is the laugh..

✦ ✦ ✦

Make any WORD a play-ground...

✦ ✦ ✦

Record an echoes
Walk it's action
Reflect it's reason
And become it's understanding

✦ ✦ ✦

Silence, the mirror of essence
How to make a second happy
Simple just be one at laugh....

✦ ✦ ✦

One can fill a room
in a sentence
call it's reason

✦ ✦ ✦

Words the eyes of reading
called UNDERSTANDING

✦ ✦ ✦

Opinion are excuses,
battery not included

Angel Ramos

✦ ✦ ✦

A pack room makes a single word..

✦ ✦ ✦

Just cause one see
A sentence in a mirror
don't mean it's a pack room

✦ ✦ ✦

Learn one, the mirror of words

✦ ✦ ✦

The finger can learn
If it take a class
From the heart….
Mirror of the tongue….

✦ ✦ ✦

Don't meter time,
Seconds are coin-less

✦ ✦ ✦

Xplore words with smile

✦ ✦ ✦

Essence, the second
Thinking, the calendar
Understanding, the experience

✦ ✦ ✦

Walk on air,
A WORD....
Wink on wind,
a sentence..

✦ ✦ ✦

To open time
One must turn
words into vision

✦ ✦ ✦

Love nothing
the beginning of everything
NOTHING AND PRESENT
ARE THE SAME IN ONE....

✦ ✦ ✦

One can pour a sentence into a word

Angel Ramos

✦ ✦ ✦

Draw the sky
as a sentence
Write the star
as a word
And be the smile
as a action

✦ ✦ ✦

Which-way, the one-way...

✦ ✦ ✦

Questions door
Answer KEY
Essence smile

✦ ✦ ✦

The door to action
is smile..

✦ ✦ ✦

Movement is a point
Action is its sentence
Essence is the word...
Create, born in words

One is the wonder in vision....

✦ ✦ ✦

Silence, the study of vision

✦ ✦ ✦

Humble the sign
signature of smile

✦ ✦ ✦

Nature the being
Flores the words

✦ ✦ ✦

Words are the ability
Present may be stage
But action clear movement

✦ ✦ ✦

Actions DOING,
how the heart write it's sentence
The word that describe the essence
IS the sentence view in vision

Angel Ramos

Hear the silence in sayin
HOW THE HEART TEACH BEAUTY

✦ ✦ ✦

If a simple can be a billboard
The sentence would be the ART work

✦ ✦ ✦

Smile are the logo of the heart

✦ ✦ ✦

Ain't nothing to sign in giving….

✦ ✦ ✦

Only smile can fill hope..

✦ ✦ ✦

Born blessing birth
Essence thinking understanding

✦ ✦ ✦

Origin smile are words

✦ ✦ ✦

Balance has one side to 2 level

✦ ✦ ✦

Before understanding,
write the sentence
In the heart…..

✦ ✦ ✦

Train a word
Become it's SMILE :-))

✦ ✦ ✦

Center, the smile sentence

✦ ✦ ✦

Love is written in a smile
 if found in words

✦ ✦ ✦

Continent, the paragraph of a word

✦ ✦ ✦

Land, the shore of smile
Believe, the recreation of words

Angel Ramos

Thought, the creation of decision

✦ ✦ ✦

Believe, how to in-power words

✦ ✦ ✦

Don't polish emotion as mirror

✦ ✦ ✦

Fear is in the wallet,
if one wants to spend on it
on emotions

✦ ✦ ✦

Fear is a looking-glass,
not a WALL...

✦ ✦ ✦

Thinking with-out understanding,
Its like saying batteries not included

✦ ✦ ✦

The mirror word
Is, the born smile

✦ ✦ ✦

Know, the one of other

✦ ✦ ✦

To color dark
One must see the light

✦ ✦ ✦

The paint of a ink
Or the stroke of brush
The art of a smile
The true words of hear

✦ ✦ ✦

Words sponsor as parent
are healthy for smile

✦ ✦ ✦

Build a word
With a sentence
The pillar smile

✦ ✦ ✦

In every word

Angel Ramos

there a sponsor call you

✦ ✦ ✦

A sentence may see the body,
but a word see understanding
Action of movement
The sentence of a word

✦ ✦ ✦

Lies don't have measurement,
it has unwanted decision

✦ ✦ ✦

Here in the center of nothing,
be is the everything of present.
Words vision in heard.
Hearing the hear of view

✦ ✦ ✦

If one are,
then is always in same.
The parallel mirror of words

✦ ✦ ✦

The how,

essence The where,
understanding The why,
thinking The what,
believe The who,
self The when, AM

✦ ✦ ✦

Lies don't have measurement,
It, has unwanted decision

✦ ✦ ✦

The Abstract is a mirror word

✦ ✦ ✦

An atom-bomb
The laugh in the heart
Before the smile in the face

✦ ✦ ✦

Just as decision has other thought
Present has essence
Understanding the maker of thinking

✦ ✦ ✦

Portion of air can give smile

Angel Ramos

How to be PRESENTS

♦ ♦ ♦

Only one can speak the words,
but understanding can do the translation

♦ ♦ ♦

Philosophy broader side is UNDERSTANDING

♦ ♦ ♦

Btful, a heart drawn by the sky
Words signing smile

♦ ♦ ♦

The true believe in present is a smile
One must vision heard to see listen

♦ ♦ ♦

Heart has two story told by same sound

♦ ♦ ♦

Sentence create thought and decision
Believe create action and movement

✦ ✦ ✦

UNDERSTANDING is the real
story teller of THINKING,
Listen is the action of hear,
Words is the believe in creation,
Born is the birth in smile

✦ ✦ ✦

Use a sentence to represent
seconds by not counting,
the always as here in IS....
repeat mirrors in words

✦ ✦ ✦

Simple is presents
as smile are adore…

✦ ✦ ✦

Religion and philosophy
      OR
Understanding as thinking
The basic of self I AM...
The words are in mirror

✦ ✦ ✦

The camel and the thought
The needle and the decision
A.k.a the big bang theory
The string theory The fractal
Or simple,
I truly AM!!

✦ ✦ ✦

Decision dries thought,
how to walk on water

✦ ✦ ✦

Don't water THOUGHT

✦ ✦ ✦

Chicken whom cross the street, decided

✦ ✦ ✦

Essence, the cement of words

✦ ✦ ✦

Dream, air with a sentence

✦ ✦ ✦

The egg is not only a chicken is a thought.

✦ ✦ ✦

A words volume is silence
To drive, is to answer

✦ ✦ ✦

If one has an idea is a meaning
If one has an present is a reason

✦ ✦ ✦

The mirror of a tear Is a planet....

✦ ✦ ✦

The chapter of a tear
Is to define a smile

✦ ✦ ✦

The goal is to smile

✦ ✦ ✦

Thinking gives
QUESTIONS ANSWERS
gives understanding

Angel Ramos

PRESENTS gives SELF

✦ ✦ ✦

Meaning is one sentence
Reason is two sentence
But one is quiet

✦ ✦ ✦

Words in essence
Are mirror in understanding
Thinking reflect their mirror
Spirit talk their walk
Movement relic
their action SELF as AM

✦ ✦ ✦

Compose a smile,
laugh at word.........
self discovery

✦ ✦ ✦

Mirror the word to be a smile......
the sentence present as SELF

✦ ✦ ✦

Essence, the smile of a hug as understanding

✦ ✦ ✦

Essence, the book of spirit

✦ ✦ ✦

talks as light
Thinking listen
as understanding

✦ ✦ ✦

Stillness, simple as A smile

✦ ✦ ✦

Myth the made-up wall

✦ ✦ ✦

Theory, the water of thoughts

✦ ✦ ✦

A finger master an arrow

✦ ✦ ✦

PERIOD OF IS
SAME AS ALWAYS
Present understanding

✦ ✦ ✦

A mirror is a word
A sentence is a reflection

✦ ✦ ✦

The sword of the smile
The shield of the HUG!!!

✦ ✦ ✦

The world as simple
The smile as it's movement

✦ ✦ ✦

Stupid for dummies
was sold-out
after beginning of Time

✦ ✦ ✦

Radio-active, a hugs-smile

✦ ✦ ✦

Essence believe
Thinking dream
Understanding GIVE

✦ ✦ ✦

Still the always,
the is in same

✦ ✦ ✦

Essence talk
Understanding translate
Thinking listen
And smiles hugs
Art reflection is mirror
words essence

✦ ✦ ✦

As one use the brush of a smile
Paint the garden
One rose can see
the pillar of an horizon

✦ ✦ ✦

Open doors of eyes,

become words

♦ ♦ ♦

TEARS, THE INK OF A SMILE

We are all a sentence
The action of a WORDS

♦ ♦ ♦

AS AIR BUBBLE
Essence understanding speak

♦ ♦ ♦

The talking MIRROR (words)

♦ ♦ ♦

Deeps nothing
Understanding above
Speak echoes

♦ ♦ ♦

Love ask
AM reach
SELF receive

✦ ✦ ✦

Air writes
the words
in wind....

✦ ✦ ✦

Air as nothing
Essence as understanding

✦ ✦ ✦

Ready...................
A word is AM
As the sentence
is the action...
The mirror reflection
of self in silence

✦ ✦ ✦

War of the thinking,
Understanding conquer

✦ ✦ ✦

Smile, the creator of simple

✦ ✦ ✦

Angel Ramos

One Is, the clear of heard

✦ ✦ ✦

One is wise, called the ear

✦ ✦ ✦

Smiles translate
what the heart says

✦ ✦ ✦

Sound carry the lyric

✦ ✦ ✦

Give, is to all...

✦ ✦ ✦

One has a space called GIViNG
Love thy words to

✦ ✦ ✦

Duty thee is thou will

✦ ✦ ✦

Love will travel in whisper essence

✦ ✦ ✦

Light is a WORD
Simple is its sentence

✦ ✦ ✦

Nothing, the billboard of a smile....

✦ ✦ ✦

Past and future
sign by present
the story of essence

✦ ✦ ✦

The pages of words are smile..

✦ ✦ ✦

Nothing is written as everything

✦ ✦ ✦

A simple can paint
the art of the HEART...
A TEAR STORY!!!

Angel Ramos

✦ ✦ ✦

Essence of the untold....tears

✦ ✦ ✦

Simple as nothing
Everything as smile
Present as create
Believe as words
Understand as think
Love as be in IS

✦ ✦ ✦

Once upon a time
Essence spoke as told…

✦ ✦ ✦

Globe the grain of a smile,
and the whole of a sentence

✦ ✦ ✦

Prototype, the meaning of REASON

✦ ✦ ✦

Smile, the paint of a sentence

✦ ✦ ✦

Nothing, a research LAB of essence

✦ ✦ ✦

STILL, IS walking

✦ ✦ ✦

Born is what
one think in understanding
believe as in words

✦ ✦ ✦

Fact is IS,
as why answer HoW

✦ ✦ ✦

The world has one point...
ESSENCE AS UNDERSTANDING...

✦ ✦ ✦

Two road is one decision

✦ ✦ ✦

Angel Ramos

Essence the maker in believe
Words the thinking in understanding

✦ ✦ ✦

WORDS PASTS present...
for now is 2omorro

✦ ✦ ✦

One can be a mirror without words

✦ ✦ ✦

SMOOTH AS SMILES ALL...

✦ ✦ ✦

The garden of a spoken sentence
Becomes the sky of the pillar WORD

✦ ✦ ✦

If a flower is the brush of a smile
Than the present is the understanding of essence HUG

✦ ✦ ✦

Beginning never ended... ask present

✦ ✦ ✦

The light of the house are words

✦ ✦ ✦

The light
will teach
the smile....

✦ ✦ ✦

Let the thinking
be the shadow,
and understanding
be the guidance

✦ ✦ ✦

As the mirror in word
Is the shine in soul

✦ ✦ ✦

Make any word smile,
and it will sail in land
The ocean of a sentence
and the wind of a word
And the movement of the heart..
How can the eye hide trust

Angel Ramos

When true is painted
by a smile as TRUTH

✦ ✦ ✦

Chemical-reaction,
a smile made by a WORD

✦ ✦ ✦

Now, are the sentence of present

✦ ✦ ✦

Don't read time as a wrist-watch....!!!

✦ ✦ ✦

Lightness and darkness,
not a balance but a thought

✦ ✦ ✦

One does create, smile walk

✦ ✦ ✦

Essence as present
Understanding as thinking
Now's as seconds

Always as IS
Believe as create
LIGHT-BULB as smile!!!

✦ ✦ ✦

Wise and hope
Must be fill with
WILL and DUTY...
The support of BORN
ESSENCE recipe
of UNDERSTANDING

✦ ✦ ✦

A hug will
give a smile
it's shine

✦ ✦ ✦

Only the WORD
will born the SENTENCE .

✦ ✦ ✦

The GODS
told the GODS,
can you hear me...
the all of a sentence

Angel Ramos

✦ ✦ ✦

Account, SELF o.k. That ALL

✦ ✦ ✦

As one walk on water...
One can walk on TEARs...
Sponsor by a smile
BOOKS, words made THEM.

✦ ✦ ✦

Science is a toy...
Watch out for the element...
Tears are salty.

✦ ✦ ✦

ESSENCE polish UNDERSTANDING,
CLEANS THINKING.
And teach words in speaking
TEXTING has no INK
EMOTION has no TEAR
Sponsor by a SMILE...
BROAD-CAST by UNDERSTANDING

✦ ✦ ✦

Pearl the silk

as shine in the jewel
emerald of the garden smile

✦ ✦ ✦

Present is the only word,
that see SELF

✦ ✦ ✦

Understanding the bridge
of ESSENCE,
where thinking center
it SELF as PRESENT

✦ ✦ ✦

Comb the sky as a sentence,
and you have the paragraph of a word

✦ ✦ ✦

IS, the everything of always,
NOW, as same in present,,

✦ ✦ ✦

Where is I, AM as IS…

✦ ✦ ✦

Angel Ramos

Present the body of words called TRUTH

✦ ✦ ✦

Motion, the sentence of movement....
understanding in thinking....
Huhh, the writer in present

✦ ✦ ✦

The heart the library of words...
a simple of AM is...

✦ ✦ ✦

Surround a sentence
with the PRESENT
of self being

✦ ✦ ✦

Choose a word
and make a master-pieces of IT
ones does it with TEARS

✦ ✦ ✦

Center balance is nothing beginning
OMG as WHY...

Wake up a smile,
as one heard a tear

✦ ✦ ✦

A tear can't out hear a smile

✦ ✦ ✦

PRESENT is the AWARENESS,
how to sign WORDS

✦ ✦ ✦

Truth, the understanding in THINKING

✦ ✦ ✦

Nothing, the canvass of creating WORDS

✦ ✦ ✦

Anybody can explain NOTHING..

✦ ✦ ✦

Mist, the clear...
Words back ground

And understanding essence
U r the leader in words

✦ ✦ ✦

BELIEVING, a word of light

✦ ✦ ✦

UNDERSTANDING, a thinking of a essence

✦ ✦ ✦

LIGHT, a smile of a sentence

✦ ✦ ✦

In every word is a smile,
simple just make it in understanding.
And be it as BORN...

✦ ✦ ✦

A split second is a balance,
now in present

✦ ✦ ✦

1st, 2nd written as ALWAYS in NOW...

✦ ✦ ✦

LIFE 1St MOMENT is BORN
LIFE 2nd MOMENT is BORN
LIFE 3thd MOMENT is ALWAYS

✦ ✦ ✦

Receive, ESSENCE as BELIEVE
BEAUTIFUL IS WONDER
IF ESSENCE IS IN BELIEVE
UNDERSTANDING the talking as THINKINg

✦ ✦ ✦

Smile is giving,
If smile learn to WALK

✦ ✦ ✦

The growth of a word
Smile the pencil...

✦ ✦ ✦

Make the pool into a sentence,
and find the word
am in it,
bet it's silence....
to wake essence in tears

Angel Ramos

✦ ✦ ✦

Yesterday is the same as tomorrow, today

✦ ✦ ✦

Tame the words
to speak in silence
as they are QUIET.

✦ ✦ ✦

Essence the view
Understanding the vision Thinking the believe
My lala-bye to I AM
Is ohh there one IS

✦ ✦ ✦

Understanding the page..
Reason UNITY
Of essence and thinking

✦ ✦ ✦

Great is thinking
Believing in understanding

✦ ✦ ✦

Renaissance of Butterflies

Love me as words
Defining sentence of AM

✦ ✦ ✦

Born to be the quality of words

✦ ✦ ✦

Time can't never be the author of smile

✦ ✦ ✦

Words before numbers
Time was never signed
Present is always free

✦ ✦ ✦

2,000 year ago moment is still, today's second
A seven key-wrench,
can't break the glass
word of the heart

✦ ✦ ✦

Us the one force...
As a sentence of always
Words parallel of smile

Angel Ramos

✦ ✦ ✦

Essence the walk of silence
An echoes in quiet
And abstract silence

✦ ✦ ✦

Nothing give the right push....
Understanding as action
Movement as believe

✦ ✦ ✦

A class with-out sentence
is not a ethical word

✦ ✦ ✦

Help is the honor of receive

Sponsoring ✦ ✦ ✦

✦ ✦ ✦

BELIEVING a smile by being words
Love the life-line of words

✦ ✦ ✦

Yes has the same
quality as no
WAIT for IT,
how balance use
quality as VALUE

❖ ❖ ❖

To run in the sentence of a journey,
1st walk in the word of a smile

❖ ❖ ❖

Movement the pen of action in present silence
I am the lecture
of your heart
called the smile

❖ ❖ ❖

Everything Xternal is inner-growth.
The teacher called Xperience

❖ ❖ ❖

Cosmos conscious
is present essence
How to build a word
As sentence in BELIEVE
A mountain was not made by grain,

it was made by patience.
And then the grain was BUILD

♦ ♦ ♦

PLEASE BE ARE.
    In IS
Where why walk!!

♦ ♦ ♦

Copy a smile the echoes of ones word
Paste a hug the reflection of ones sentence

♦ ♦ ♦

Written, the eyes of vision

♦ ♦ ♦

If one chapel is a smile,
what sentence as
brick would one USE..

♦ ♦ ♦

The entity of origin is essence

♦ ♦ ♦

The origin of a speak is present

✦ ✦ ✦

The water of essence
Is understanding
Planting words in thinking
And letting believe
Be the creator
Of its nurture growth

✦ ✦ ✦

Just as human live in earth,
words live in human...

✦ ✦ ✦

The shower of a shine
Is the echoes of the smile

✦ ✦ ✦

The reflection of a mirror
is the I AM of the words

✦ ✦ ✦

A sword is the light of the smile
that is the shield

Angel Ramos

✦ ✦ ✦

For the eyes can read the sentence of I AM.
The words chapter as message in VISION

✦ ✦ ✦

Eyes can be the book
Tears can be the pages
But smiles are it's truth message

✦ ✦ ✦

Listen to the words
Saying in I Am.

✦ ✦ ✦

The glass of the words are it's smile,
be careful of the sentence
that can be turn to stone

✦ ✦ ✦

Words mirror of words
Are the saying of I AM

✦ ✦ ✦

If one teach words silence

Silence will teach words presents

❖ ❖ ❖

To guide a smile
It's the sentence giving

❖ ❖ ❖

All and all is everything always.
The present as now

❖ ❖ ❖

Now, is the pen of present

❖ ❖ ❖

Ones past and future
is the sentence of present

❖ ❖ ❖

One talk,
but don't see
the vision behind it
Made a tear into a duce-wild,
if not tape a joker in its sleeve

❖ ❖ ❖

Angel Ramos

WILL HERE IS THERE IN WHERE
PRESENT UNDERSTANDING
IS NOW IN ESSENCE

✦ ✦ ✦

Word the leader as sentence
Word the pillar as anchor
Word the understandin as thinkin
Word the creator as believe
Word the essence as LOVE

✦ ✦ ✦

1ST MIRROR EVER SEEN,
BABY SMILE AFTER THAT
IS NOTHING BUT POLISHING

✦ ✦ ✦

THE SMILE IN THE GLASS
STRAIGHT SENTENCE OF A WORD

✦ ✦ ✦

REMEMBER, IS A MIRROR
FAVORITE A SMILE..
ESSENCE LIGHT

✦ ✦ ✦

love for respect
respect for value
VALUE for LOVE

✦ ✦ ✦

if a word was a cup
what light would one give it

✦ ✦ ✦

EARTH ECHOES IS A SMILE...

✦ ✦ ✦

Ask a word a joke,
but be careful of it's laughter

✦ ✦ ✦

A word can teach
another word smile,
look at me for
I am your sound.
The chapter called silence

✦ ✦ ✦

Train the words new tricks,
the one fill with tears

Angel Ramos

Sign me your mirror QUEST
And I will reflect Present of now's silence

♦ ♦ ♦

Why say in reading nothing,
nothing the page of experience present.
NOTHING THE PROPHERCY OF NOW

♦ ♦ ♦

Noise don't have weight in tears,
it has smile in essence

♦ ♦ ♦

A ocean is a body
A sea is a body
Now let put think into play
A BODY is a ESSENCE
Battery not included,
jus SMILE

♦ ♦ ♦

Write my smile,
become your echoes.
AM ASK SELF

♦ ♦ ♦

Believe the creator of words,
but one build balance
The mirror of echoes...
hearing words in silence

✦ ✦ ✦

BASE CONTEXT is COMPLEX PERPLEX...
how to draw a sentence into smile

✦ ✦ ✦

SIMPLE, CARRY SMILE only

✦ ✦ ✦

BEING, AREA IS AM...

✦ ✦ ✦

Words have passage
call so-call journey
The route about self

✦ ✦ ✦

Let's read a full
empty cup of water
A world of a question
Is the answer to the story

Angel Ramos

✦ ✦ ✦

Star sing as shine in sang
Light live in essence as believe

✦ ✦ ✦

Love, the billboard of the HEART
The sign signature,
the art of a smile

✦ ✦ ✦

SMILE, THE ERASER OF TEARS

✦ ✦ ✦

If water can break
a rock with patience
That mean a smile
 can heal
a hug with love

✦ ✦ ✦

Implement in BELIEVE,
jus a sentence
as of ESSeNCE

✦ ✦ ✦

BRING THERE,
called the SMILE

✦ ✦ ✦

Only tears have the reflection of the world
But a smile has the mirror of words

✦ ✦ ✦

LIFE, the jewel of a smile
Lecture knowledge is smiles HUG
The acknowledgement of love PRESENT

✦ ✦ ✦

Keep survive out of, live

✦ ✦ ✦

THINKING IS THE BIG
AS BANG IS THE UNDERSTANDING
Myths THEORY
Or yet the word of a sentence.....
BELIEVE as ESSENCcE

✦ ✦ ✦

Love string is the sentence of the smile

Angel Ramos

♦ ♦ ♦

A song is sang
as a sentence
A tree is look
upon as a smile

♦ ♦ ♦

Simple is written
in understanding,
not in thinking.
See thinking is in words,
understanding is in sentence
as in spelling
a word BORN BIRTH

♦ ♦ ♦

A song is sang as a sentence
A tree is look upon as a smile

♦ ♦ ♦

Don't create nothing
Create everything that start with
nothing as a sentence

♦ ♦ ♦

Love string is
the sentence of the smile

✦ ✦ ✦

Decision is a word
Thought is a sentence
A smile is a WORD...
A thought is a HUG

✦ ✦ ✦

An un-scribe word is a tear sentence

✦ ✦ ✦

One can't be human
One can only be words

✦ ✦ ✦

A smile is written in words

✦ ✦ ✦

Bliss the blanket of the eyes
Mist the story of the tears
Essence the understanding of the thinking
Grace the truth of the words

Angel Ramos

✦ ✦ ✦

All direction in one decision

✦ ✦ ✦

Perplex, how to knit wonder...
Simple un-twine the fantasy

✦ ✦ ✦

Funny how one, draw a universe into a page

✦ ✦ ✦

Simple, the single as SAME..
One as mirror of all

✦ ✦ ✦

The parent word
is the student sentence

✦ ✦ ✦

There, to learn in teach...

✦ ✦ ✦

Let paint the smile as words

Renaissance of Butterflies

✦ ✦ ✦

One can only draw
philosophy with understanding
Post a sentence in any word,
sprinkle love into it.
And one just become
AM of choice

✦ ✦ ✦

CURATOR of the words is a SMILE

✦ ✦ ✦

Bliss the sky-writer of nothing....

✦ ✦ ✦

As the words as guide,
Yea yield in thinking

✦ ✦ ✦

Now, the simple
sentence of present,
as one

✦ ✦ ✦

Angel Ramos

There is no shadow in LOVE...
smile pillar

♦ ♦ ♦

Nothing thin line is the light
The sentence as center
And words as present
A smile is the SHADOW of hugs...
Post a sentence in any word,
sprinkle love into it.
And one just become
AM of choice..

♦ ♦ ♦

Survive is not a sentence....
Now live is a REASON.

♦ ♦ ♦

Live is made...
Survive is ones chose

♦ ♦ ♦

Love the brush-pen-pencil of a smile

♦ ♦ ♦

A word, the map...
A sentence, the compass
A chapter, the mark...
A book, the essence...

✦ ✦ ✦

Don't say can't in will...

✦ ✦ ✦

The writer of a reading is the smile...

✦ ✦ ✦

Darkness, the light searcher
How one looks for present

✦ ✦ ✦

A word the teacher of a sentence....
And the student of the thinking

✦ ✦ ✦

Galaxy universe
Hugs smiles

✦ ✦ ✦

Angel Ramos

Only self can see
a shadow sentence,
that represent AM

✦ ✦ ✦

Genius or wisdom has
no power over SIMPLE.
A pond's reflection

✦ ✦ ✦

DONT MAKE WORK
AS ERASERS,
they have a life TOO
Don't give a sentence
If it don't have words in it...

✦ ✦ ✦

Love wonder to see,
if it found in words

✦ ✦ ✦

CERTAIN IS...

✦ ✦ ✦

Can one read a blank-page...

O.k. Now put a word in IT
The study of essence...
that how creation is form

✦ ✦ ✦

if words were a cave
the encryption would be the sentence

✦ ✦ ✦

Thinking is a TOY
Understanding is the battery
ESSENCE IS THE JOY!!!

✦ ✦ ✦

Venture to words
Is learn to how
to see it's sound
Essence teachin in
understanding as thinking

✦ ✦ ✦

LOVE, THE PENCIL OF A SMILE

✦ ✦ ✦

Humm a words

Angel Ramos

hear it's sound
as one looking at it...
is the products of AM

✦ ✦ ✦

Words aren't DARK...
Sounds as present
Volume as NOW

✦ ✦ ✦

If one can hear the pain...
One must learn to hear essence
It's voice is the smile

✦ ✦ ✦

The known in heard
Silence own page
Vision present of WORD

✦ ✦ ✦

If one can catch a tear
One just caught the world...

✦ ✦ ✦

KAO'S, AN ILLUSION WORD

Wise don't fit in simple,
give it a second.
So one can apply the understanding.

✦ ✦ ✦

Let nothing settle,
when applying simple..

✦ ✦ ✦

teach a sentence
  one word
to open its world

✦ ✦ ✦

every word is the mirror of now
Present as the pond of view
Understanding words in glance

✦ ✦ ✦

where, the there of here as now

✦ ✦ ✦

one never left there

✦ ✦ ✦

Angel Ramos

Simple, the simple by words,
you are their guidance

✦ ✦ ✦

start never finish....
If words love thy,
mirror them back.
They have rights too.

✦ ✦ ✦

the true line is a smile

✦ ✦ ✦

Words say hello in self

✦ ✦ ✦

Every single word has the story of love in one BOOK.......self

✦ ✦ ✦

Reason corrects meaning
As understanding sponsor thinking

✦ ✦ ✦

I hear your text....

Hear in heard
Present as see
Sang as told
And seen as view

✦ ✦ ✦

The language of thinking is UNDERSTANDING

✦ ✦ ✦

Reason corrects meaning
As understanding sponsor thinking
A sentence is the circle
As the link is the words

✦ ✦ ✦

As vision explain
View heard....

✦ ✦ ✦

SIMPLE STRONG, movements action in silence.

✦ ✦ ✦

A SMILE CAN WATER the LAUGHTER

✦ ✦ ✦

Angel Ramos

ONES IS THE NUTRITION of WORDS,
the planted seed

✦ ✦ ✦

THE MOMENT.....
think now,
are you applyin understandin

✦ ✦ ✦

The world is a BOOK,
with each own sentence

✦ ✦ ✦

Love is so fine AS it IS,
don't add thinking to it.
ADD understanding.
The sign sword in the ROCK
called words

✦ ✦ ✦

SHADOW present called past,
the guardian

✦ ✦ ✦

The eye of a book of words

called one sentence

✦ ✦ ✦

For a smile that shine, the star is fulfill

✦ ✦ ✦

The page of a cup...
let that sink in the
blank spot of nothing

✦ ✦ ✦

An ant can carry a sentence,
as a word become A mountain

✦ ✦ ✦

One can fit BAD in Good,
if one choose TOO...

✦ ✦ ✦

Why the only answer in balance

✦ ✦ ✦

Words don't have blanked,
unless it wanna cover it's self in shine

Angel Ramos

✦ ✦ ✦

As a tie is to a suit
The words are to UNDERSTANDIN

✦ ✦ ✦

All direction is ones point...
That-ta WAY :-)

✦ ✦ ✦

Cold and hot
is yes and no
as water and AIR

✦ ✦ ✦

Everything gather in a words is btful...

✦ ✦ ✦

What glow in a words
is a sentence

✦ ✦ ✦

If love is ART, then a smile is a painting

✦ ✦ ✦

NOTHING, the story of silence...

✦ ✦ ✦

An atom is a life ROAD
If a mirror is a sentence
Make sure the words
match the reflection

✦ ✦ ✦

Don't cross the bridge,
if the words don't have sentence

✦ ✦ ✦

Water is clear,
not a sentence.
The power of words essence

✦ ✦ ✦

Keepin everythin btful in the war-fare system....
the library of emotions

✦ ✦ ✦

Mind, the pillar build by words

✦ ✦ ✦

Angel Ramos

Words the road map of smile

♦ ♦ ♦

Words are words
We are jus the example

♦ ♦ ♦

Tears not included

♦ ♦ ♦

A two way word, has one understanding
Words are the birth of a sentence
words are the context of understanding

♦ ♦ ♦

Light of essence
Purpose opportunity

♦ ♦ ♦

Decision as a thought
Love as a sentence
Conquer ALL
Believing in words
Essence creater
Self as AM master ALL

✦ ✦ ✦

TOLD HAS A MISSION called HEARD

✦ ✦ ✦

The quality essence give are spoken words,
giving by vision and told by silence

✦ ✦ ✦

For in water, there is a sentence..
For in AIR, there is HARMONY..
For in ESSENCE, there is LIFE.
For in SELF, there are WORDS..
I in AM,
Mirror is the record
Vision is the sound
Understanding is the HARMONY

✦ ✦ ✦

Copy is the repeat words reflect in silence

✦ ✦ ✦

If one teach love,
the words will say I AM

✦ ✦ ✦

Angel Ramos

A sentence, can draw
The word of the picture

✦ ✦ ✦

Don't let a line be the present..

✦ ✦ ✦

YOUR SMILE IS THE POWER OF CREATING

✦ ✦ ✦

LOVE ART IS SMILING,
as brushing words in UNDERSTANDING

✦ ✦ ✦

Love is made by the words is giving,
in the sentence describe the words

✦ ✦ ✦

Give one a door, and draw the key as a sentence
The big-bang theory
or the fractal of myth,
it's simple to just say
a decision of a thought.
Or the no of yes,
the balance of a word

✦ ✦ ✦

Political is a decision split in half....

✦ ✦ ✦

Space the non-movement of silence present

✦ ✦ ✦

DARKness has A word call LOVE, fish it

✦ ✦ ✦

A gold of a word is the sentence of the smile

✦ ✦ ✦

A word can be a book,
as a sentence can be a library

✦ ✦ ✦

One can find a grain in a mountain
One >CAN< find a sentence in the eyes

✦ ✦ ✦

Thinking is the page as the walkin silence

Angel Ramos

✦ ✦ ✦

I can make one THINK
If one ready to learn understanding

✦ ✦ ✦

Nothing the pocket of life....

✦ ✦ ✦

The moon is the shadow of the SUN
The star are the sentence
And earth the essence as creation

✦ ✦ ✦

A tree smile, is the whistling wind

✦ ✦ ✦

Wonderful is the keeper

✦ ✦ ✦

For ones told
Begin GROWS

✦ ✦ ✦

Control smile the journey

♦ ♦ ♦

Why waste, what is giving in nothing

♦ ♦ ♦

The mystery of a word is a smile,

just ask the sentence♦ ♦ ♦

♦ ♦ ♦

The wages of emotion are TEARS
The value of a smile is its SHINE....

♦ ♦ ♦

Strength as strong the protector of a smile....

♦ ♦ ♦

If one hold a cup in silence,
fill it in SENTENCE...

♦ ♦ ♦

Quench the words,

Angel Ramos

thirst the understanding

✦ ✦ ✦

Silence the movement, thoughts sentence

✦ ✦ ✦

Reflection as A paragraph,
chapter UNDERSTANDING

✦ ✦ ✦

For one is the born in the words call smile

✦ ✦ ✦

As essence walk the light
Smile stand and shine as reflection

✦ ✦ ✦

Walk words in eyes silence

✦ ✦ ✦

Humble, the spoon will feed one

✦ ✦ ✦

DOMAIN, A CASTLE IN WORDS

✦ ✦ ✦

The weight of water is a feather in TEAR....

✦ ✦ ✦

The suits of men and women,
will not fit the tie of ESSENCE.
Spirit is An office within it SELF......
UNDERSTAnding

✦ ✦ ✦

PAST IS MOMENTS
FUTURE IS ACTION
UNDERSTANDING IS PRESENT
MOVEMENT SILENCE

✦ ✦ ✦

The action of words is understanding
The thinking of understanding is SMILiNG

✦ ✦ ✦

One is gather in a sentence, as words

✦ ✦ ✦

Angel Ramos

Wonder the vision in view as words

✦ ✦ ✦

Open the eyes of words,
UNDERSTANDING

✦ ✦ ✦

There is ONCE UPON A-TIME call NOW!!!!

✦ ✦ ✦

Time is not a second
Time is not a minute
Time is not a hour
Time is not a month
Time is not a year
Time is not a map
Time is the heart <3

✦ ✦ ✦

Ocean air
Wave winds
ESSENCE WORDS

✦ ✦ ✦

The tree in the forest, ask for help.

As the words of thinking do TOO...
understanding shine on them as pillar,
the sentence as smile

✦ ✦ ✦

The tree in the garden,
is the same as the flowers

✦ ✦ ✦

Air is to nothing,
like words to essence.
Ask the wind,
it tell it's story same
as the waterfall told IT

✦ ✦ ✦

One AM understAnding
The essence thinking awakening

✦ ✦ ✦

If one drink WATER
Is it the right paragraph...

✦ ✦ ✦

Reason meaning, is a SMILE

Angel Ramos

❖ ❖ ❖

Heard, the why in here

❖ ❖ ❖

Silence, sound is action

❖ ❖ ❖

A smile, the still movement

❖ ❖ ❖

IS, the word of NOW
ESSENCE UNDERSTANDING as THINKING PRESENT
WORDS of BEING in AM
SELF REFLECTION as MIRROR

❖ ❖ ❖

Onion and lemon will make the eyes CRY
Thinking and understanding will make essence live

❖ ❖ ❖

If thinking gave you understanding,
grow a lemon tree....
essence asking words to listen

✦ ✦ ✦

Growth, the sentence of thinking as understanding

✦ ✦ ✦

master of words am in silence

www.ingramcontent.com/pod-product-compliance
Lightning Source LLC
Chambersburg PA
CBHW070050080526
44586CB00013B/994